The Which? Guide to
Domestic Help

About the author

Lynn Brittney, who has worked in public relations, publishing and as a lecturer, has written articles for various magazines and journals as well as several books. She is the author of a Which? Consumer Guide on working from home. Her other books include a series of Directors' Guides for the Institute of Directors, *Intelligent Manufacturing* (Addison Wesley) and *Successful Conferences and Other Business Events* (WEKA Publishing), and, for Foulsham, *Study Time Management* and *A Woman Alone*.

The Which? Guide to Domestic Help

Lynn Brittney

 CONSUMERS' ASSOCIATION

Which? Books are commissioned and researched by
Consumers' Association and published by
Which? Ltd, 2 Marylebone Road, London NW1 4DF
Email address: books@which.net

Distributed by The Penguin Group:
Penguin Books Ltd, 27 Wrights Lane, London W8 5TZ

First edition September 1998

A catalogue record for this book is available from the British Library

ISBN 0 85202 743 5

For a full list of Which? books, please write to Which? Books, Castlemead, Gascoyne Way,
Hertford X, SG14 1LH or access our web site at www.which.net

Cover and text design by Kyzen Creative Consultants

Typeset by Saxon Graphics Ltd, Derby
Printed and bound in Great Britain by Clays Ltd, Bungay, Suffolk

Contents

*An asterisk next to the name of an organisation in the text indicates that the address can be found in this section

Introduction

As we approach the end of the twentieth century, the demand for help in the home – which for decades after the Second World War was at a comparatively low level – is once again running high, despite the fact that we live in a very different sort of society. A large percentage of people now have more money, but less time, than ever before. The role of women, in particular, has changed, from homemaker to money-earner, and most of them work away from home. As a result, a vast army of support services has gathered in recent years to provide services in the home to hard-pressed working women, busy single men, affluent seniors and the housebound.

The term 'domestic help' no longer adequately describes what is now a highly specialist and varied range of home services. Of course, there is still a thriving back-bone of domestic cleaners who turn up once a week and 'do through', often for cash-in-hand. Increasingly, however, workers in the domestic employment sector, particularly in the emotionally fraught areas of childcare and care of the housebound elderly, are trained professionals, working within a framework of government regulations.

While such qualifications and regulations provide some degree of reassurance to employers, these alone cannot guarantee that the relationship between you and the carer, housekeeper or nanny you have employed will be a harmonious and mutually satisfactory one. Bringing someone into your own home to work for you – and perhaps to live there 24 hours a day – is an especially sensitive employer/employee situation. The individual foibles you can tolerate in a workplace, and from which you can escape at the end of the day, may become unbearable if you are sharing your home life with them. Employing the wrong person for your household can lead to disappointment, resentment, anger and despair, as evidenced by the numerous tales that circulate of inadequate or otherwise unsatisfactory nannies, nurses, housekeepers and carers. Finding the right person to suit your needs and budget can often be frustrating – and even if you find someone to fill the bill, it may not be easy to persuade that individual to choose you.

On the other side of the coin, domestic employment agencies have a fund of horror stories about unreasonable and, occasionally, unpleasant employers. Those who are fortunate enough to have found their ideal employer/employee relationship rarely talk about it, for fear that a desperate friend may try to poach their paragon by offering better terms and conditions.

As this book will show, a positive approach to recruiting and employing home support services *is* possible, but it requires thorough preparation and research. Knowing exactly what you want before you approach an agency, place an advertisement or interview a candidate should take you 50 per cent of the way toward selecting the right person. This means assessing your needs, budget and family demands carefully at the outset, and to check and double-check the terms and conditions in contracts between you and the agency or you and the employee. You need to understand the rights of everyone concerned and, just as important, what can be done if things do not work out.

If you have not employed a nanny, housekeeper or carer before, the business of how to find candidates and then to assess the applicants can be daunting: this book aims to put you in a stronger position to make an informed choice.

In a working relationship that depends for its success on individual personalities, there can be no guarantees, but this book should put you in the best position to avoid the problems. It will help you to clarify your options, plan and prepare constructively, and stop you from rushing headlong into an arrangement that could cost you dear, both emotionally and financially.

Chapter 1

The resurgence of the home support industry

Domestic help is now as large an industry in the UK as it was just before the Second World War. The two main reasons are the role of women – changed from that of housewife and carer to that of paid employee or business proprietor, usually working outside the home – and the disappearance of large family units in which family members cared for each other's children and elderly relatives. Therefore, the greatest need for help in the home has been in the 'care' sectors – for the very young and the very old.

Demand for other types of domestic help has increased too. Many people with a career and a fair amount of disposable income require, and possess the means to buy in, assistance with cleaning, laundry and even cooking, when necessary. Large numbers of working couples and single parents have to have someone to look after their children on a regular basis. Elderly people are also employing more domestic help, either because they need support in the home or simply to free up more leisure time.

Recent years have seen a trend towards earlier retirement and, with the benefit of substantial occupational pensions, many early retirers are able to take full advantage of their leisure and are happy to pay someone else to do the household chores. People are also living longer but with the advancement of age may require assistance from carers to enable them to stay in their own homes for as long as possible.

All of these factors have contributed to the resurgence of the domestic employment industry. A survey by the research group Mintel, published in January 1997, shows that the amount spent on domestic staff in the UK has quadrupled in the last ten years, to an estimated £4.3 billion a year, compared with £1.1 billion in 1987.

Throughout this book short real-life examples ('case histories') have been provided to illustrate the different ways in which people use domestic help, its advantages to them, what it costs them and, in some cases, what action they have taken when the arrangement did not work out as well as they had hoped.

Working women

Statistics from sources such as the Institute of Employment Studies and the Equal Opportunities Commission★ show that, by early 1994, one in six working people in Britain was a woman with a child under 16 years old. In other words, 4.3 million working women have dependent children. And half of all women with children under the age of ten go out to work.

This presents a logistical problem. A very small percentage of those working women will have unpaid domestic support – for example, an unemployed husband who does the housework and looks after the children, or a mother, mother-in-law or sister who performs the domestic/caring function. Even assuming that a proportion of those working women are 'superwomen', who work by day and perform all the domestic chores in the evening when the children are in bed, childcare remains an issue. Very few jobs fit in with children's school hours. Even teachers have to be at work before their children arrive at school, and frequently leave work some time after the children have gone home. Childcare needs to be organised for school holidays and, in recent years, staff training days (which give most children at least two days off from school a term); in addition, all parents face the ever-present risk of children being ill and having to stay at home for days, even weeks, at a time.

It is no surprise, therefore, that the biggest growth area in support services has been in the childcare sector. In 1986 some 64,160 registered childminders in the UK provided 137,732 places for children. By 1996 this had risen to 103,000 registered childminders providing 376,000 places, an almost threefold rise. Despite this, an acute shortage of places persists. Those who cannot place their children with a childminder have to find places in day nurseries, employ nannies or au pairs, or make arrangements for their children to go to someone else's home.

Demand shows no signs of diminishing. In 1986 approximately 45 per cent of women who had worked during pregnancy returned to work within 11 months of giving birth. By 1996 this had risen to 67 per cent.

Apart from the working women with dependent children, many women who are single, childless or whose children have left home lead busy working and social lives and have little time, or inclination, for housework. They represent the section of the community most likely to employ domestic staff in some capacity – say, a twice-weekly cleaner, someone to do the washing and ironing, a gardener or handyman.

Single parents

In 1975, according to research conducted by the Equal Opportunities Commission, 90 per cent of families in the UK were headed by a married or cohabiting couple. By 1995 that figure had dropped to 78 per cent and is dropping faster each year. The percentage of families headed by a lone mother increased in the same period from 9 per cent to 20 per cent. Statistics in this area are somewhat misleading, because a significant number of 'lone mothers' claiming benefit fail to admit that they are in fact cohabiting and have not been found out. Nevertheless, the percentage of unattached women giving birth has risen and the divorce rate remains very high (affecting two in every five marriages).

Although the government is endeavouring to make it more cost-effective for parents with dependent children to go out to work, the initiatives proposed will need to be matched by a massive increase in quality daycare provision for children if they are to be of real value to families. Among the initiatives announced in the 1998 Budget was the Working Families Tax Credit (WFTC). Under the WFTC, which should come into effect in April 1999, a tax credit will be granted to the value of 70 per cent of eligible childcare costs up to a ceiling of £100 per week for one child and £150 per week for two or more children.

CASE HISTORY: Geraldine

Single and in her 40s, Geraldine lives in south-east England, works long hours and does a great deal of travelling for her job, staying away from home for one night or more each week. Her part-time housekeeper comes in three times a week to clean, wash and iron for her, do a weekly shop and look after the cats. She works an average of 16 hours a week and Geraldine pays her £5 per hour.

Care of elderly and disabled people

The issue of providing care for the elderly and disabled makes the childcare problem almost pale into insignificance. The number of people who care for elderly relatives in the UK is almost twice the number of working women with dependent children – 7 million (roughly 3 million men and 4 million women) compared with 4.3 million. According to Age Concern, approximately half of these carers are aged between 46 and 64, which means that a large proportion of them work outside the home as well as fulfilling the role of carer.

CASE HISTORY: Harriet

Harriet, a divorced mother of two children who lives in the West Country, is in her late 30s, suffers from multiple sclerosis and is finding it increasingly difficult to cope with household tasks. As her ex-husband provides her with a generous maintenance (but no practical support), she receives minimal Social Services help and relies in the main on private services. Social Services provides someone to bathe her three times a week (just one carer, as she is not wheelchair-bound) and, until recently, provided a home help who did some housework. Owing to budget cuts that service was withdrawn, so Harriet now pays approximately £80 a week to a local woman who cleans, cooks and irons. Harriet also subscribes to a personal emergency alarm system so that she can summon help should she need it during the night or when the children are at school. Because children are involved, the Social Services department is obliged to monitor the situation continually. Harriet does not go out in the evening so she does not use the services of a babysitter, but she has an arrangement with a friend to take her children, unpaid, should she be ill or have an appointment away from home.

The costs in emotional, financial and health terms to carers who are family members have not been calculated, but the costs to industry have. Research published in 1997 by the Institute of Employment Studies showed that approximately 5 per cent of UK employees take one day's sick leave each month in order to care for a dependent relative. Conservative estimates suggest that this costs employers in excess of £50 million annually. Of course, no one could perform the function of carer and work part- or full-time without some assistance from others. The Department of Health's community care statistics for 1996 showed that, in an average week, 491,000 households received home help or home care services.

A survey of almost 2,000 carers carried out by the Carers National Association★ revealed that nearly 95 per cent were the spouse/partner, son, daughter or parent of the person cared for. Only 20 per cent of those carers were in employment and most of those were part-time. Almost 50 per cent of the carers had savings below £3,000.

The statistics relating to carers show only part of the picture, however. A great number of elderly and disabled people who have health or mobility problems, or are housebound, do not have a relative to care for them. Most wish to remain independent and in their own homes for as long as possible. But it does mean that they are entirely reliant on outside help, from whatever source.

Over 10 million people in the UK today are over 65 and this age group is forecast to increase steadily over the next ten years. People are living longer, and most proprietors of residential homes say that the average age of their clients has risen over the last decade from 70-something to 80-something.

Residential care of the elderly can be even more of an emotive issue than childcare. The decision that an elderly person should go into residential care is often put off for as long as possible. Organising a reliable and satisfactory domiciliary care situation is frequently difficult because the elderly are, quite rightly, concerned about where they live and how they live.

Since the introduction of Care in the Community, when Social Services departments throughout the country were totally re-vamped, elderly and disabled people and their carers have found that it has become increasingly expensive to buy the services many of them require. Social Services departments have a duty to provide, either themselves or via other organisations, help in the home for those deemed to be in need. The assessment process is often harsh. An applicant for help will be assessed on the basis of physical need – for example, inability to get out of bed, wash, cook for themselves, feed themselves – and financial situation. As every Social Services department has its own assessment criteria and its own financial constraints, generalisations about what an 'average' department would provide in the way of a 'care package' or reliable guidelines as to what would class a person as needy enough to receive state-funded care are of little use. Sometimes, an elderly person can be quite severely disabled but because he or she is comfortable financially the local Social Services will simply provide a list of private agencies, which charge a considerable amount for care services.

CASE HISTORY: Rose

Rose, aged 78, lives with her unmarried daughter in a house in Central London. Her daughter works full-time in the City. Rose has a heart condition and is quite frail but the Social Services department was unable to offer practical help because of the level of Rose's income. Although her daughter's income is not allowed to be assessed, it was undoubtedly a factor in the final decision. Therefore, Rose and her daughter have to employ a carer through a private homecare consultancy. Following the consultancy's free assessment of Rose's needs, a carer has been provided for five days a week to perform services such as light housework, give Rose a bath and prepare a midday meal. A carer also escorts her if she needs to travel to a medical appointment and the consultancy can provide someone to sleep overnight or even stay for a week if Rose's daughter has to go away on business or needs a break. What Rose pays each week varies according to the help she needs. Standard personal care is approximately £8 per hour, while domestic care is nearly £10 per hour. If someone is required to stay the night while her daughter is away it costs about £45 per night (there is a £15 surcharge if the person being cared for requires assistance more than three times during the night. For someone to stay a whole weekend costs in the region of £200.

As Age Concern★ observed in its 1996 discussion paper 'Challenge on Care':

> These niceties of funding, and distinguishing between health and social care, are completely meaningless to the average citizen. How can it be logical to treat a stroke patient in hospital for free, and then to discharge that patient into the community where the long-term disabling consequences must be managed by the individual, the family or the Social Services authority on a means-tested basis? Or where incontinence, which seems at face value to be a medical issue, can only be managed in one's own home if the equipment and support services are paid for?

Support services, however, may not be available. As Help the Aged★ reported in November 1997 in its paper 'A Life Worth Living':

> Access to the services and support that older people need if they are to remain independent is steadily whittled away. The pattern of erosion is widespread. The numbers of people who receive home care have been cut – down 4 per cent in 1996 and 5 per cent the year before . . . Domestic help from Social Services, including cleaning, has all but disappeared, in spite of its importance to health, self-respect and personal dignity. And it is often difficult for older people to get small household jobs and repairs done, such as changing light bulbs or washing curtains. It is not clear how older people who can no longer do household tasks are supposed to manage, unless they are in a position to employ private help, or there is a local voluntary organisation which offer these kinds of services.

We tend to think of older people as being relatively comfortable financially nowadays. Indeed, among the present 55–70 age group those who accumulated sizeable occupational pensions do seem to be enjoying a golden era. But those who are older than 70 are in a different position. According to Age Concern, 'Only one-third [of older people] have enough income to bother the Inland Revenue, and those falling into the higher tax rates are negligible. The same pattern applies to capital savings and investments. . .'

A recent trend has been capital release, sometimes called property reversion plans or extra income plans, whereby elderly people sell their homes to financial institutions in return for a sum of money, less than the market price of the property, and the right to live in that house until they choose to leave or they die. The capital released by the sale of the house is used to pay for the occupant's care and support within it. Capital release schemes are usually available only to home owners over the age of 70; in the case of a couple, both would usually have to be over 70.

A very recent development has been care insurance policies, which some financial services companies are trying to sell to people now in their 50s. They work rather like private medical insurance: provided you are in good health and fully mobile when you take out the policy, should you become in need of care after paying only one premium you will be eligible to claim on the insurance to cover some of your care needs. As for most medical insurance policies there is a ceiling on the amount of money that the policy releases each year. This amount is dependent upon the premiums paid and the continuing care circumstances.

Those elderly people who live with their carers fare little better than those who live on their own. A report by the Carers National Association entitled 'Better Tomorrows' states:

> Payments made by carers for services vary widely. One in 4 [of the carers surveyed] are in households getting free services from Social Services. Nearly another quarter are getting nothing from Social Services and paying at least £5 a week for services. About 1 in 5 carers – mainly those in employment and higher income households – are paying both Social Services and privately for services. Over 10 per cent of carers paying for services privately spend on average more than £20 per week. Those getting services from Social Services for which they are charged pay from under £3 to over £20 per week.

Care of the elderly has become big business, as the growth in the number of private agencies that specialise in staff that fulfil carer and nursing functions in the home shows.

CASE HISTORY: Emily

Emily is 86 years old and lives on her own. Her income consists of a widow's pension and some other state benefits. She has no children. She has chronic arthritis and is partially sighted so she finds many tasks very difficult. Although she can get herself in and out of bed, wash and dress herself, she can no longer cook for herself, clean the house or iron clothes. She is fortunate to be living in Northumberland, which has the largest publicly funded home help department within Social Services, attending to more than 4,000 households a year. Emily's home help comes every day to do some cleaning, ironing or other small jobs in the house, make Emily a midday meal and prepare a meal which Emily can put in the microwave in the evening. For this service she pays a standard charge per week of £12, however many hours are worked. If she has an emergency and has to call for extra help, the charge does not vary; on the other hand, it must still be paid if Emily goes away for a few days. The charge is set every year and usually goes up in line with inflation.

Like other Social Services departments, Northumberland stipulates the conditions of service of home helps in a contract with the client. These include tasks that home helps are not allowed to undertake – for example, they must not climb anything which is unsafe or administer drugs by injection. They also relate to the home help's behaviour in the client's home – for example, the home help must not borrow anything from the client, smoke in the client's house or bring children to work with her.

The cash-rich, time-poor market

A further significant boost to the growth of the domestic service industry comes from the well-off. A survey carried out at Coventry University in 1996 showed that the average salary of the top 1 per cent of earners in London and the South-east was £164,000, and concluded that these people were contributing to the growth not only of the 'servant' market but also of small companies and freelance operatives who provide ancillary domestic services from one-off cordon bleu catering to people who do specialist shopping on a client's behalf.

The upsurge in the demand for domestic servants by high earners seems to be widespread. A 1997 report in the *Irish Times* spoke of a growing need among high-earning Irish families for 'house-managers' – a house-manager being 'a dynamic person who does it all': lives in, cooks and keeps house, works roughly 40–45 hours a week and earns up to £250 per week plus food and possibly a car.

Young professionals in UK cities spend a good deal of money on domestic help. One agency quotes the example of a 25-year-old money broker in London who said he wanted someone to do everything his mother did for him when he lived at home. Once the agency had established that this did not include bathing him or wiping his nose, it was more than happy to provide someone to cook, clean, iron, shop, sign for the post and deliveries, pay the milkman, organise repairs and decorating, and attend to every other practical domestic detail of the young man's life.

CASE HISTORY: Charles

Charles is a high-earning barrister aged 32, unmarried and living in London. His live-out housekeeper manages his home completely: she shops, cooks, cleans, does the laundry, makes the beds and even pays some of his household bills. Charles also employs a gardener who comes in for one full day a week to keep the small garden looking immaculate. When he wishes to entertain, his housekeeper contacts a small catering company, which cooks the food, prepares the table (complete with table decorations) serves the meal and washes up afterwards. Charles pays his housekeeper £200 a week and gives her a housekeeping budget of £150 per week, for which she produces a weekly account. The gardener costs £40 a week and the catering company's charges vary depending upon the size of the dinner party and the complexity of the menu.

Another agency reports that the number of full-time servants employed by very wealthy families has risen over the last few years from four to five. Whereas households formerly hired a cook/housekeeper, a nanny, a chauffeur and a gardener, such families now separate the role of cook from that of housekeeper.

As more people retire early, some while still in their 50s, and take advantage of the many leisure and travel opportunities available, the rise in the employment of casual domestic help, particularly in rural areas, has been significant. However, several domestic staff agencies in regional areas complain that many people find their help through the 'black economy'. As one agency head put it, 'Fewer people are coming to us looking for domestic help because they are all employing local people to do their cleaning and gardening and paying them cash in hand.'

One comparatively recent phenomenon has been the rise of the house-sitter and the pet-sitter (see Chapter 9). It has become increasingly common for people to take several holidays a year, at which times arrangements have to be made for pets and to protect the house from burglary. Hence the need for professional sitters; with a sitter, beloved pets no longer have to be uprooted from their comfortable homes and put in draughty kennels where they pine away and maybe catch some virus from their close contact with other pets; and houses do not have to be left empty and property unguarded, tempting the local criminal fraternity, while their owners are away on holiday. Sitters are the ideal solution, provided they are properly vetted and their contract provides for compensation for the home-owner if things go wrong.

CASE HISTORY: Roger and Ellen

Roger used to own three shops selling computer equipment and Ellen used to be a school secretary. Both have retired, in their mid-50s, with good private pensions and considerable savings. They recently bought a holiday home in Tuscany and spend a fair amount of time there each year, as well as taking other holidays. An agency provides them with a twice-weekly cleaner, who also does the laundry. The agency also provides a house-sitter whenever they are away. The cleaner costs them about £30 per week and the agency charges £100 per week for the house-sitter.

A further service, for pets, has emerged, as the advertisements in any vet's surgery in the country will confirm: dog-walking. All sorts of dog-owners, from the elderly whose mobility has become restricted to the busy working family, feel guilty about their animals not getting enough exercise, so they pay someone to walk the dog once or twice a day. Some enterprising individuals are even offering a complete pet care service which encompasses dog-walking, feeding pets when the owners are working long hours, pet-sitting and taking animals to the vet when necessary.

Self-employed people now offer services such as ironing (either done in the client's home or taken away); complete provision, maintenance and replacement of indoor plants and floral arrangements; catering at home for dinner parties, buffet parties and children's parties; steam cleaning of your entire home (walls, carpets, upholstery etc.) when you are on holiday, have just moved out of a house or are about to move into one; specialist cleaning on the spot of furniture, fabric-covered walls, valuable soft furnishings; and temporary assistance at home doing all housework and childcare during the difficult period after giving birth. These small businesses have successfully tapped into the market comprised of those with money who want to buy greater flexibility, a bit of comfort and make more of their leisure time.

CASE HISTORY: Peter and Diane

Peter, an international financier, and Diane live in a large house and entertain a lot. They used to employ a cook, a housekeeper, a nanny, a chauffeur and a gardener, but now that their sons are at boarding school they no longer need a nanny. The housekeeper and chauffeur live in, the cook, who works from 11 a.m. until 2 p.m. then returns at 5 p.m. and works perhaps as late as 11 p.m., lives out. The gardener lives out and works every day from 9 a.m. until 5 p.m. The house and grounds are so large that the housekeeper employs two cleaners and the gardener employs an assistant. All the staff are from agencies and the annual staff bill is approaching £100,000.

In the chapters that follow, this book will help you work out what sort of arrangement you need to suit your own requirements and point you in the right direction for finding the help you need.

Chapter 2

How to find suitable help

In the currently booming domestic help industry it might seem that there is no shortage of people and services to call upon. However, as most people will tell you who have ever tried to find a reliable nanny, rejected umpteen au pairs before finding one they would want to share their home with, or tried to organise care for their elderly mother, finding the individual that really suits you, or your relative, with the right personality, qualifications and experience, can be an uphill task. Regulations that cover caring are at best patchy. Children, for example, have greater protection under the law if they are sent outside the home to be cared for than if they are cared for by someone in their own home.

Before embarking on a search for domestic help, look carefully at all of the options available.

Childminders

Although professional childminders do not fall within the scope of this book as they do not work in people's homes (and certainly would not consider themselves to be 'domestic help'), the childminding option is briefly covered here because it offers children far greater protection under the law than some of the alternatives and may be worth considering even if, as a parent reading this book, your current view is that you must have your offspring looked after at home.

If a childminder looks after children below the age of eight she has to be registered with Social Services, her home environment is subject to regular inspections, a police check is done on the childminder and her family's background, and she may need references from a doctor, and possibly others. The Children Act 1989 imposes limits on the number and ages of children she may look after during a day. These numbers must include her own children if they are not at school. She may look after no more than three children under the age of five and only one may be under 12 months old. Alternatively, she may look after no more than six children under the age of eight, of which no more than three are under the age of five. Moreover, Social Services will usually set a limit on the number of children over the age of eight. The childminder has to keep proper records pertaining to each child and must be able to contact a parent in case of an emergency. Most childminders have public liability insurance; indeed, some local authorities have made it a compulsory requirement. If a child in her care has an accident, however minor, the details must be written down – what happened, when, and what treatment was given – and the incident fully explained to the parent; the parent must sign a form saying that he/she understands that it was an unavoidable accident and that all appropriate help was given. Childminders are encouraged to join the National Childminding Association,★ which regularly updates its members on safety, educational play, activities, and so on.

On the emotional side, a child gets plenty of one-to-one attention in a secure home environment, with a regular routine and, possibly, the company of other children. Childminders will usually take their charges out to local playgrounds and give them a normal daily routine both in and outside their home so that they take an active part in the local community. This, of course, is valuable if you choose a childminder who is local to your home rather than one who is local to your workplace.

One disadvantage is that if your child is ill the childminder may elect not to take him/her until the child has recovered sufficiently to pose no risk of infection to the other children in the childminder's care.

Childminders are paid £2–£5 per hour, depending upon where they live in the UK (Greater London being the most expensive area). Weekly rates vary from £50 to £300. For more specific guidance on childminding rates, contact the National Childminding Association.

Nannies

Nannies can either live in (in which case they need their own room with a television, and some will expect their own bathroom and use of a car), or out (in which case they need to be very local). Nannies may work for more than one family at a time, as described below.

A nanny does not have to have formal training; nor does she have to be registered with Social Services or checked out by them (unless she cares for children from more than two families). Anyone can call herself a nanny and anyone can set up a nanny agency. The fact that a nanny comes to work in your own home makes it a private arrangement and, as such, not covered by the law unless an incident occurs that warrants police, Social Services or other official intervention.

The government is examining the feasibility of a national register of nannies, as well as regulations to control the setting up and operation of nanny agencies.

A Mintel survey published in 1997 revealed that there were then 100,000 nannies working in the UK, but some organisations claim that the actual figure is probably much higher, perhaps as high as 200,000, because a great number of 'nannies' are employed under casual cash-in-hand arrangements that are not recorded anywhere.

Trained nannies, of course, are in demand internationally and their salaries reflect this. Nannies who have trained at the Norland★ and Princess Christian★ colleges can command upwards of £200 per week. Many other places offer childcare training, however. Local colleges, for example, offer childcare courses leading to a recognised qualification.

Most nannies hold the NNEB Diploma in Nursery Nursing, awarded by the Council for Awards in Children's Care and Education (CACHE),★ which takes them two years to achieve and involves a high proportion of practical work, usually in hospital maternity units or crèches, though some colleges, like Norland, put their students out on work placements for a few weeks during each summer. CACHE also offers the following awards: NVQ in Childcare and Education, NVQ in Playwork, Certificate in Childcare and Education, Diploma in Nursery Nursing and Advanced Diploma in Childcare and Education (ADCE).

Other childcare qualifications include the BTEC National Certificate/Diploma in Childhood Studies (Nursery Nursing), City and Guilds childcare courses, National Association for Maternal and Child Welfare (NAMCW) certificate and diploma courses, Pre-School Learning Alliance (PLA) courses and the London Montessori Centre's Montessori Childcare and Teaching Diploma. Some nannies have trained as nurses.

All the courses are based on the care and development of very young children, children's behaviour, play and practicalities such as feeding and physical care, with other modules that will depend to some extent on the emphasis of that particular qualification – education, nursery nursing or whatever.

To employ a nanny with no, or minimal, qualifications is to take an enormous risk, although qualifications on their own do not ensure suitability. Certainly, anyone in charge of a small baby or a pre-school child should have qualifications. Ideally she should also belong to a professional organisation such as the Professional Association of Nursery Nurses,★ which provides its members with information relevant to their jobs on a regular basis. This organisation is campaigning for a legal requirement that no one is allowed to call herself a nanny unless she has one of three recognised qualifications: an NNEB Diploma in Nursery Nursing, a BTEC Diploma in Nursery Nursing or an NVQ Level 3.

A prospective nanny who claims to hold any of these qualifications should be able to describe in some detail what modules her course comprised, what sort of practical work she did, and where, which aspects of her training she found most interesting and how long it took her to qualify.

Nanny agencies

The Federation of Recruitment and Employment Services (FRES),★ an organisation which represents employment agencies and has a specialist nanny section, recommends that all its member agencies should meet each nanny and check all her qualifications and references before putting her on its books. It strongly supports the view that no one should be allowed to call herself a nanny unless she holds a recognised qualification.

None the less, many staff agencies do not fully check or even interview all the applicants that they put forward for jobs (see Chapter 4), so for the time being the onus is very much on the parent to check out the qualifications and references of any prospective childcare employee.

Nanny-sharing

Nanny-sharing is a useful arrangement for parents with, perhaps, one or two children, for whom the expense of a full-time nanny could not be justified, particularly if one of the children is at school for most of the day, or if a parent works part-time. Nanny-sharing can work in several ways. For example, the nanny can reside in one household looking after a couple of children and another household's children can be brought to her for the day. Alternatively, the nanny could live out, working mornings in one household and afternoons in another. Another scenario might be for her to look after one household's pre-school children during the day and add another household's school-age children to her responsibilities for the after-school hours. However the arrangement works, the costs are shared and many parents find this a convenient and cost-effective arrangement.

CASE HISTORY: Callie

Callie, an unmarried mother with two young adopted children, runs her own business from home, making designer knitwear. She shares a qualified live-out nanny with a neighbour, another single mother, who has one child and works full-time out of the home. The nanny, a local girl in her mid-twenties, still lives at home. As Callie's house is larger than her neighbour's, the nanny looks after all the children there. Callie remains in her work room for most of the day, but occasionally comes out to have a break and see the children. The nanny takes the children out, sometimes using Callie's car, which she is insured to drive. Callie does her own housework and gardening but employs a babysitter twice a week in the evenings when she goes to her gymnasium. For the nanny service Callie pays about £120 per week, which represents just over half of the nanny's salary. The sum was agreed by the two mothers taking into account the fact that the childcare takes place in Callie's house. The other mother contributes food towards the children's weekly meals.

Au pairs

Au pairs are often teenage girls who are between school and higher education (but may be older – say, up to 27), who take the job to gain experience of living in another country and often to learn the language of that country, while looking after children, doing a little housework and receiving in exchange board and lodging plus some pocket money. In practice, many who come to Britain have limited command of English and less childcare experience. To use them as a cheap alternative to proper childcare is irresponsible.

Au pairs are not intended to be cheap nannies. However, they are useful for looking after children of school age who need only to be fed in the mornings, taken to school, picked up in the afternoons and looked after until a parent gets home; or, alternatively, for looking after children of mixed ages if one or other parent is at home or works from home and can be on hand immediately in case of a problem.

According to one of Europe's largest au pair agencies, approximately 20,000 au pairs come to London each year and twice that number come to stay with families in the south and south-east of England.

Au pairs' working conditions are regulated. For example, an au pair from within the European Union must have her own bedroom (and, preferably, bathroom, although this is not a legal requirement) and all her food provided. She is allowed to work a maximum of five days (37 hours) a week, performing duties such as childcare and light domestic chores. She is entitled to have two days off a week and time off to attend English classes if required. An allowance of £35–£55 a week is usually paid. Au pairs from non-EU countries may work only for a maximum of 25 hours per week. Visas for au pairs are normally issued for a 12-month stay, but can be extended to the maximum allowed, which is two years.

The fact that au pairs have a limited work permit is another reason why they should not be used as full-time childcare. For children to have their carer changed every 12 months is very disruptive for them. Children of all ages need some continuity in this area of their lives.

Employing nannies/mothers' helps from overseas

Most of the agencies that deal with the placement of au pairs also deal with English-speaking nannies and mothers' helps from countries such as South Africa, Australia, New Zealand and Canada as well as from Europe. These women come to work in the UK on a 12-month working holiday visa, which allows them to work full-time for 12 months. Again, they are not an ideal solution for a family unless its childcare needs are coming to an end.

Agencies provide nannies from the above-mentioned countries who they claim will be experienced but not necessarily qualified, and will have at least two work references. Agency nannies can be placed in sole unsupervised charge of children and will help with domestic chores. A mother's help, on the other hand, is likely to be younger, with some childcare experience but no formal training. Agencies recommend that a mother's help does not have unsupervised care of children, but she will help with childcare and perform domestic chores. A nanny's live-in salary ranges from £120 to £200 per week. A mother's help's live-in salary ranges from £80 to £100 per week.

Paying a friend to provide childcare

If someone comes into your home to look after your children, she does not have to be qualified or registered to do so. Likewise, if you take your children to someone else's house to be cared for, for a period of up to two hours a day only, that person does not have to be qualified or registered either.

Many people may feel that a friend who is herself an experienced mother would be a perfectly suitable childcarer. If you feel that the person is trustworthy, competent and caring there is nothing to stop you making a mutually beneficial financial arrangement for childcare. It must be emphasised, however, that you do so at your own risk. No arrangement, even if it is with a close friend, should be without a proper written contract, agreed by both parties, not least because without it you would have no redress in law should something go wrong (see Chapter 6).

Where to find home childcare

Childminders

Childminders are registered with the local Social Services department, which can supply a list of all the registered childminders in your area. Sometimes local doctors' surgeries and health centres will have lists, and baby clinics always do. The best way of finding a good childminder is by word of mouth, but check that she is registered before entering into any agreement. The local Pre-School Playgroups Association will be familiar with most of the childminders in the area as it probably delivers and collects several of their charges. Mother-and-toddler groups will know most of the childminders and may also use them. Your problem will not be finding good childminders: it will be finding a spare place with one of them because they are in such demand.

Nannies

Finding a good nanny requires a rather more intensive search. There are plenty of agencies, most of which advertise in magazines such as *The Lady*,* where people have advertised for domestic servants for over a hundred years, *Country Life* and *The Tatler*, or any of the publications which are aimed at people with the income and lifestyle to support a fully trained nanny. But these agencies do not just service the top 10 per cent of the population; they have more modest childcare packages on offer. The advantage of going to an agency is that it will offer choice. The disadvantage is that the agency fee can amount to one month's worth of the nanny's salary (which could be as high as £800): this may be acceptable if the first nanny you employ turns out to be a good choice, but extremely expensive if you have to keep starting new ones every few months.

It is advisable to ensure that the agency you use is a member of FRES, whose members work to the organisation's guidelines (see Chapter 4). Ask anyone you know who has used an agency successfully to recommend one to you.

Depending upon your circumstances, it could be worth asking around locally to see whether anyone would be interested in nanny-sharing before you opt for finding a nanny solely for your household.

A good source of nannies is the training colleges themselves: not just the well-known uniformed 'nanny schools', but also the local colleges that run childcare courses. If you have the time and your children are adaptable enough, you could offer to have a trainee to do her work-experience stints in your house, but this is not recommended for the care of infants. One of the advantages of going to the colleges is that you should be able to talk frankly with the course tutor to find out which students have the best attitude and are the most responsible.

You could place an advertisement for a nanny in one of the magazines mentioned above or in a specialist or trade publication such as *Professional Nanny*★ (see Chapter 4). If you do, be prepared for an avalanche of applications, depending on your location and the terms of the position you are offering.

Sometimes people looking for a position advertise locally. Nannying occasionally attracts trained nurses who want a break from the National Health Service, and they often advertise in local shops and newspapers as live-out nannies. Those with maternity nursing qualifications can be ideal for the care of babies and toddlers.

Au pairs

Au pairs are usually found through au pair agencies, the best of which maintain contact with the girls throughout their placements and even organise regular social events where they can meet other au pairs in a central location. That way the girls feel less isolated in a foreign country. The agency you choose should be a member of FRES or the International Au Pair Association (IAPA).★ The best agencies will do their best to match your needs with someone who appears, on paper at least, to be suitable, but if you end up with the wrong person entirely you can only send her back and try again.

Another way of finding an au pair is through a friend whose own au pair might be able to arrange for her sister or a friend to come over to be your au pair. There is no guarantee, however, that the sister or friend will be of the same calibre as your friend's au pair, and this method of recruitment can be rather hit-and-miss.

Several of the larger nanny/mother's help/au pair agencies now advertise on the Internet. These advertisements are useful because they give a great deal of detail about the agencies – far more than an advertisement in a publication. For reasons of security, no reputable agency should allow details of the individuals held on its books to be scanned and/or downloaded by anyone: the advertisement should simply be a point of contact. Only after a proper application has been made to the agency, and has been thoroughly checked out, will you be sent full details.

Eldercare and care of disabled people

The first point of contact for arranging help at home should always be the local Social Services department, whose responsibility it is to assess the requirements of all elderly clients requiring assistance, regardless of their financial position. The department's experience in the day-to-day needs of the elderly and disabled will enable it to investigate all the care options thoroughly, and perhaps think of some needs that may otherwise have been overlooked.

The system works in two ways. Firstly, anyone can approach Social Services and ask for an assessment to be carried out. An elderly person can ask on his or her own behalf, or someone can do it for them. This could be simply a concerned neighbour, but it must be with the permission of the person concerned. Social Services staff may not enter anyone's home uninvited, unless that person is at such extreme risk that a doctor has called them in.

The other route for assessment is via a hospital social worker. This commonly happens when an elderly person who lives alone is about to be discharged from hospital but may not be able to cope without support once back home again. In such cases the hospital social worker is called to the ward by the nursing staff and is given a medical assessment of the patient's condition. He or she then has to talk to the patient (or, to use the department's terminology, the 'client') and/or any relatives or persons acting on behalf of the client and arrange to visit the client's accommodation to assess the situation.

A financial assessment, or means test, is usually undertaken and Social Services recommends to the client and/or relatives a care plan detailing the level of care required for this person to be able to live comfortably at home, what the Social Services department itself can provide and what will have to be obtained privately. The department has all the relevant information about local private care agencies and can suggest a care package that draws in services from different agencies.

A care package can cover the following:

- nursing attendance (over and above the normal once-or-twice-weekly district nurse attendance, which is organised through the GP's surgery)
- personal care (bathing, washing, assistance in going to the toilet,

assistance in getting out of bed in the morning and going to bed at night, hair washing, shaving, administering prescribed medication other than injections etc.). These can be undertaken by non-nursing staff

- making meals, preparing delivered meals or helping to feed the client
- coping with children (in the case of a younger disabled person)
- doing the laundry and ironing
- doing incontinence laundry, emptying commodes, providing incontinence pads
- providing apparatus to make certain tasks easier
- doing the shopping
- doing light housework and odd jobs (no heavy lifting, climbing, electrical or plumbing repairs)
- teaching the client new skills to enable him/her to do certain jobs
- linking the client up to an emergency alarm system
- reading to a partially sighted or blind person and dealing with their correspondence
- garden maintenance
- collecting pensions and banking money
- respite care (whereby a client spends one or two weeks in a residential unit to give the full-time carer a break)
- domiciliary respite care (a carer takes up residence in the client's home to provide cover whilst the full-time carer is in hospital or away for some other reason).

The care package may draw upon Social Services, voluntary organisations, charities and private agencies to supply any part or all of the package. Every care package is individually tailored to the client's requirements and budget and costs will vary enormously, but an example of rates charged by one Social Services department is as follows: those with savings of £16,000 or more will pay the full charge of £8.44 per hour (this is the full charge for services provided directly by one specific Social Services department; where an independent care provider is used, the charge will vary); those with an income of more than £212 per week but savings of less than £16,000 will be charged a maximum of £5.08 per hour; those with savings and income below the quoted figures but savings of more than £10,000 or an income of more than £125 per week (unless income support is received) will be charged £5.08 per hour for up to five hours to a maximum of £25.40 per week; additional hours are free of charge. Those who receive income support or have savings of less than £10,000 and an income below £128 per week will generally pay nothing at all.

For those tasks that are within the capabilities of the average person it is, of course, possible to pay a friend or neighbour rather than approach Social Services. But a person who is severely incapacitated, requiring a great deal of assistance to do the simplest tasks, will need experienced professional care.

The agencies that provide these services have to ensure a certain standard of care. FRES has a Nurses and Carers Agency and can provide a list of members. The United Kingdom Home Care Association★ represents private care agencies which all abide by the Continuing Care Conference Guidelines (see Chapter 4). FRES recommends that each agency's induction/training programme should include the following:

- confidentiality
- communication
- feeding
- first aid
- food hygiene
- handling of money (for clients)
- recording and reporting
- moving and handling (of clients).

FRES also recommends that all agency carers should have 12 months' previous experience in a recognised care setting. A code of practice for agencies supplying care staff has been established by FRES to ensure that the services offered by members are of a high standard and to protect the interests of users of care services. The code includes sections on assessing a carer's competence and suitability, and information to be provided to both carers and clients.

One of the disadvantages of the present domiciliary care system, and the one that distresses the dependent elderly the most, is that the individuals providing the services come and go with alarming frequency. It is not possible for most care-package clients to establish a relationship of trust and familiarity because they never see the same person on a regular basis. This can be extremely hard when the service being performed is a highly personal one, such as bathing or dealing with incontinence.

Many charities and voluntary organisations offer extra services such as getting and returning library books; home decorating; pet care; transport to and from hospitals, shops and theatres; special outings; chiropody; hairdressing; shopping; and provision of equipment, such as wheelchairs.

Most elderly people shrink from approaching Social Services for assistance, taking the view that it is an undignified and humbling experience to have to admit that they can no longer cope on their own. Many, unaware that government policy since the late 1980s has been to avoid putting people into residential care, are frightened that if they make contact with Social Services they will be put in a home. The financial aspects can also be distressing. Many elderly people do not like to reveal their personal financial details to strangers, and it can be frightening for them to realise that domiciliary care may cost them a lot of money in the long term.

The fortunate elderly are the ones who are in robust health and simply want some straightforward domestic help. They can find a reliable person through a friend or neighbour or go to a domestic service agency to get their twice-weekly cleaner – though even that may not be straightforward (see Chapter 4).

What Social Services will provide

A local authority has a duty to provide assistance in certain circumstances. For example, the Chronically Sick and Disabled Persons Act 1970 requires a local authority to provide services if a person is:

- substantially and permanently handicapped
- blind or partially sighted
- deaf or hard of hearing
- mentally ill (this includes diseases such as Alzheimer's)
- mentally handicapped.

Services that a local authority must supply which come under the care-in-the-home heading are:

- provision of practical assistance within the home
- provision of disability aids and equipment

- assistance with adaptations to the home
- provision of meals at home or elsewhere (for example, you could be picked up each day and taken to a day centre where you would be looked after and fed)
- provision of, or assistance in getting, a telephone or any special equipment necessary to use a telephone.

Each local authority will have its own code of practice or quality standards formulated for the provision of domiciliary care services

The quality standards issued by East Sussex Social Services are shown here as an example because the department has one of the largest elderly populations in Britain. The purpose of the standards is to ensure that every home-care 'service user' in East Sussex is provided with a consistent, reliable and professional service. They are the minimum standards that all organisations providing home care services in East Sussex must meet in full.

Responsibilities to service users
All staff and home-care workers will show respect for:

- the service user and her/his wishes regarding how services are provided
- the service user's home and possessions
- the service user's chosen lifestyle
- the service user's privacy.

Where the service user receives services from more than one home-care worker, the organisation shall identify a 'named home-care worker' who will act as the service user's main point of contact and attend service reviews.

Organisations shall ensure that there is a continuity of home-care workers allocated to each service user, whenever possible, taking into account sickness, holidays and change of staff. They will also minimise cancellations and disruptions to established patterns of home-care service and will give service users prompt notice of known changes.

Organisations shall ensure that service users and home-care workers are matched effectively, taking into account the service user's age, gender, cultural and religious beliefs.

(see box below for an example of one Social Services department's quality standards). The code or standards are used mainly to ensure that the service providers contracted by the Social Services department to perform domiciliary care services operate to a level of service acceptable to the department. Social Service departments now rarely provide many such services themselves. Your local Social Services department should be able to provide you with its own code of practice or quality standards, which will give you an idea of the standards governing the operation of the service.

Organisations will not normally require their staff to be responsible for service user's money or keys unless this has been specified in the care plan and the service user is in agreement.

Information

Organisations shall give service users written information, in plain language and in a format accessible to them, about the home care being provided. The information must include:

- details of the named home-care worker and that person's supervisor
- emergency contact number(s), including the Social Services department's emergency duty team where necessary
- information on how to comment on and complain about home-care services
- information about how records are kept
- the organisation's brochure describing its aims and home-care services
- precise information about when home-care services will arrive.

Staff training and procedures

The East Sussex quality standards also cover the recruitment, training and support of home-care workers employed by the organisations undertaking the work on behalf of the Social Services department. A section on practice and procedures deals with supervision and recording of medication; keyholding practice; handling service users' money; dealing with emergencies; risk assessment/safety inspections, and other matters relating to the well-being of both service user and home-care worker.

A final section on quality assurance outlines the requirements for monitoring and reviewing a service and a complaints procedure.

CASE HISTORY: Samuel

Samuel's elderly mother lives on her own nearby and has become increasingly housebound. After finding advertisements for home-care consultants on the Internet, Samuel asked some of them to visit and give a free assessment of his mother's needs. He chose not to involve Social Services at this stage as his mother has a substantial income and he knew that a friend of hers in a similar situation and with similar income had been turned down by them. In any case, Samuel was prepared to contribute towards his mother's care.

The consultants recommended that certain adaptations be made to the house (such as a stairlift and rails for the bathroom and toilet) and two consultancies provided care plans for Samuel to consider. He chose the more expensive one, which amounted to nearly £200 a week, because he was able to negotiate a clause in the contract which stated that, whenever possible, barring unforeseen circumstances, the same carers would be provided each week to perform the personal care tasks required. His mother has a bath twice a week, which requires one person to assist; she also has a cleaner twice a week and a daily visit from a carer who prepares a hot meal at lunchtime and a cold meal for the evening.

Domestic help

The only regulations that affect domestic staff are general employment regulations and those covering the employment of overseas workers or illegal immigrants. Other than that, a 'shift-for-yourself' culture prevails. However, the more reputable agencies operating in this sector will adhere to a code of practice, such as that stipulated for members of FRES.

As with nannies, au pairs and childminders, the only sure way of getting a reliable and hardworking cleaner, gardener, window cleaner or any other domestic service is by personal recommendation from a friend. The local 'woman who does' and the jobbing gardener/handyman stand or fall on their reputations. It is in the area of specialist staff that you may need to resort to agencies and advertisements, in which case you are in the same situation as the nanny-hunter.

If you are well-off and searching for a cook or a butler, you could approach the cordon bleu colleges or butler schools, who will recommend some of their students to you. The only problem with this is that, according to the principals of several well-known cookery schools, domestic service ranks very low on the career scale of most trainee cooks, who would prefer to be chefs in large hotels or restaurants or run their own businesses. Butlers, by the very nature of the job, intend to go into domestic service but most of them want to go overseas where they will be paid substantial salaries by wealthy Saudis or Americans.

Housekeepers or house-managers are in great demand but, according to several agencies in Ireland, where demand has reached crisis point, young people do not want to do the job and all the experienced middle-aged women housekeepers have been snapped up. The 'servant problem' that first hit Britain after the First World War is now being experienced by the high earners of the 1990s.

At the top end of the scale, the specialist cooks, housekeepers, chauffeurs, gardeners, butlers, valets and personal maids are still available but may well lack experience and skill. Agencies exist to cater to this market but report that it is becoming increasingly difficult to find British nationals who have experience of top-level domestic service. A large proportion of the staff on their books are from overseas, particularly the Philippines, Thailand, South Africa and other African countries, and the Middle East – anywhere, in fact, where servants are still employed as they were in pre-war Britain. Agencies which specialise in servants from overseas say that the only difference between employing foreign workers as opposed to British nationals is that it is usually written into the employment contract that the employer will provide a free return air ticket each year to allow the employee to visit his or her family at home.

Those who need domestic help but have more limited resources have to make do with assembling a variety of local services which fulfil all their domestic help needs. This may be someone who comes in to clean a couple of times a week; someone else to do the laundry and ironing (or a collection service for the same tasks); a local man/woman who mows the lawn once a week and tidies up the garden; a freelance caterer who comes in as required to prepare special dinner parties and events; or a local woman who comes in to prepare a special dinner party or event and stays to wash up afterwards; a local girl who acts as part-time nanny to the children; an agency that provides house- and pet-sitters when the family goes on holiday; a one-man/woman business providing an odd jobs and decorating service; a local car-hire firm that provides chauffeur-driven cars for special events or important business clients; a specialist firm that comes in every six months to steam-clean the upholstery and the carpets; a window cleaner who comes once a week; and so it goes on. A whole army of domestic help can be assembled from different sources – usually local advertisements, personal recommendation or word of mouth.

In America this part of the service sector has become known as 'domestic outsourcing' and has been taken to the ultimate level. Just as one can hire a wedding consultant to organise a wedding and co-ordinate all the services, so one can now hire a consultant who will put together a 'domestic outsourcing package', in other words, assess a client's total domestic help needs, purchase all the relevant services and manage them on a day-to-day basis – for a substantial fee, of course.

In the UK it is possible, if you have the money, to pay an estate agency or property consultant to manage the maintenance of your house as though it were a rented home. For a fee the company can organise cleaning, gardening, window cleaning, repairs, pool maintenance and interior decoration, leaving you free to enjoy your home without the hassle of managing the services.

CASE HISTORY: Colin

Colin's old school friend Daniel, who lives locally, is a freelance property manager who looks after and maintains rented properties on behalf of clients. As Colin is often away on business and has little time to organise domestic help while he is at home, he pays Daniel to do it for him: the help comprises a weekly cleaner and gardener, in addition to which Danial inspects the property regularly, deals with any repair work and pays an agency to house-sit whenever Samuel is away for more than three days. Daniel is paid a monthly fee of £200, out of which he pays the cleaner and the gardener, who cost £35 per week, and £65 is put by for repairs each month, whether needed or not. House-sitters charge according to the size/length of the job and Colin pays that bill himself.

Another trend originating in the United States that could well spread to the UK in due course is the employment of what are, in effect, freelance personal assistants. Described elsewhere as a '21st-century Jeeves', the personal assistant will perform a wide range of duties for busy employers who do not have the time to manage all areas of their lives themselves. Charging $25–$30 (approximately £17–£21) per hour and supported by a mobile phone, pager, car and access to the Internet, the assistant will undertake anything from sorting out cupboards, filing and making travel arrangements to booking theatre tickets and shopping.

However, before you ring an agency, draft an advertisement or ask a friend of a friend how much she pays her domestic helper, you need to be very clear about the sort of person you need and what you want him/her to do for you. The parameters are broad, as Chapter 3 reveals.

Chapter 3

The domestic employee's role

Ninety years ago the duties associated with domestic service positions were common knowledge: no elaboration was necessary when one advertised for a housemaid, as everyone applying for the position knew exactly what being a housemaid involved. Today, the duties and responsibilities of a domestic employee vary enormously from household to household and are defined only on the basis of a negotiated agreement between employer and employee.

The key factor in a successful working relationship is for each party to understand the other's requirements, from the beginning. You must decide what functions and responsibilities you want your employee to undertake, and your employee must understand fully what is expected of him or her and agree to it.

Deciding what you want is not quite the same as deciding what you *need*. The gap between them is often an economic one: what can you afford? Personality considerations must also be taken into account: the carer or nanny has to be not only competent and affordable, but likeable and sympathetic too. This is particularly important if the employee is to live in.

Assessing care for children

Children need a stable environment, no matter how resilient they seem. Most children can cope with their parent(s) working full-time and being available only for short periods as long as the rest of their life is well ordered and secure.

In assessing the best type of care for your children the first consideration is their ages. If you have pre-school children and you have decided to have them looked after at home rather than take them to a childminder or day nursery, you will need to consider employing a qualified nanny. It is repeatedly stressed in this book and by professional organisations in the field of childcare that the responsibility for infants and toddlers should not rest with an unqualified or inexperienced carer.

Children of primary school age also need experienced care, especially when they first start school. The first year of school can be emotionally and physically draining for many children. They may go to school each morning filled with fears about the day ahead and come home so tired that they can barely manage to eat their tea. The first few years in the playground can be a rough experience, with many accidents requiring the attentions of the school nurse or even the need to be picked up and taken home. The first few years of school and the close proximity of so many other children can mean coughs, colds and other viruses brought home to be shared with the rest of the family.

Working parents who have just reached the school stage with their first child can easily underestimate the demands that primary school children make on their parents. In addition to coping with illnesses and accidents, parents of young children are often expected to devote time and effort to their education and to school activities. As well as events to attend, there is reading to be heard and small amounts of homework to be supervised before the children go to bed, thoroughly tired, at a time when you might perhaps still be travelling home from work.

Children of secondary school age are less demanding in some respects. Parents may be able to reduce their level of participation in school activities, for example. Problems at school and the need for someone to talk to when they come home do not diminish, however, and may even increase with the additional school work and social pressures of this age group.

Before any decision can be made about whether a nanny, au pair or mother's help should be live-in or daily, you will need to make an accurate assessment of the hours required, duties and responsibilities of the carer for your children.

Assessing hours of attendance

When assessing the hours that you want your children's carer to work, be realistic about the hours that you work yourself and add on travelling times and an allowance for traffic or other transport problems. If you work full-time and commute some distance, at what time do you leave home and at what time do you return? If flexibility on the part of your nanny is important – to cover for unexpected late meetings, times when your child is unwell and cannot attend school, or regular commitments outside normal office hours, for example – this will need to form part of the employment contract.

In addition to being realistic about the hours when childcare is essential, consider whether an hour or two of extra cover at one or both ends of the day would help the household to run more smoothly. For example, if you leave home at 7 a.m. with barely enough time to get yourself washed, dressed and fed, do you need someone to feed and dress the children between the hours of 6 a.m. and 8 a.m.? Similarly, if you return from work at 7 p.m. and rush to prepare the children's supper, bathe them, get them ready for bed and so on, consider keeping the nanny for an extra half-hour or hour to perform some of these tasks so that you can unwind for a short period before reading the bed-time stories and putting the children to bed.

At the other end of the scale, if you work part-time, or work from home, and your children are all of school age, you may just need someone to take your children to school in the mornings, collect them in the afternoon and look after them for a couple of hours until you take over at about 5 p.m. If your children are teenagers who can get themselves ready and off to school, a part-time housekeeper who works afternoons and supervises your children until you get home may be all you need.

Responsibilities of your children's carer

Be very clear at the outset about the role you want your nanny, mother's help or au pair to play in your children's lives. Do you require a nanny to take your place completely during the working week? For example, do you want the nanny to attend school functions, take your children to the dentist or doctor, attend to your baby during the night, take your children out to buy new clothes or shoes and so on? Or do you want the nanny to care for the children's personal and transport needs during the week while you make special arrangements to be there for doctor, dentist and school appointments and buy their clothes, shoes and other items at weekends?

If you want the nanny to be a surrogate mother to your children, be very clear about where you draw the line. If, for example, the school wishes to discuss your child's bad behaviour or poor homework, do you decide that, as the nanny is responsible for your child's behaviour and usually supervises the homework, that she should go to the school instead of you? Will you give the nanny total responsibility for dealing with problems that arise while you are at work, or do you want her to contact you at such times to allow you to make the decisions?

Do you require a nanny to act, in some measure, as a housekeeper too, performing tasks such as shopping for food, doing the laundry and ironing, and cleaning the children's bedrooms? Or do you want her to limit her responsibilities to direct supervision of the children, providing everyday care and some basic education through play?

If you have an au pair to help you, her duties must be clarified, too. Do you want her to vacuum the carpet every day, dust, gather up the dirty washing from everyone's rooms, do the washing and ironing, and play with the children? Do you also want her to transport your children or your elderly mother to and from appointments and social events? If so, you will need someone who has experience of driving on British roads. Remember that an au pair legally may not work more than five hours each day, five days a week.

Live in or live out?

If your work means that you are absent from the house for an average of 12 hours every day, or you frequently need evening babysitting or night-time care, you will probably have no choice but to engage a live-in nanny as it will be difficult to find someone who is be prepared to travel to your house each day to start work at 7 a.m. and stay late every evening or most evenings. You must also keep in mind the number of hours you can reasonably expect your nanny to

Sample job description: live-in nanny

- get the children ready for school in the mornings, supervising washing and dressing and preparing breakfast, and dress the baby
- take children to school
- take care of baby during the day, providing stimulating play, preparing feeds, taking for walks in fresh air etc.
- collect children from school and give them tea
- supervise any homework as necessary before allowing children to play/watch television
- take responsibility for all children's medical and social appointments e.g. dental appointments, baby clinic, children's parties (deliver and collect), playing with friends after school (deliver and collect)
- organise children's outings during school holidays.

Sample job description: mother's help

- arrive at 8.30 a.m. to take children to school and finish at 12.30 p.m. (parent working part-time will collect children from school)
- during the morning, do whatever housework is necessary, including laundry and ironing
- supervise, as necessary, sick child who cannot attend school (in such circumstances overtime will be paid from 12.30 p.m. until 2.30 p.m., when parent finishes work).

Sample job description: housekeeper

- look after home from 9.30 a.m. to 4 p.m. Monday–Friday, doing all housework, laundry and ironing, dealing with dry-cleaning, supervising and paying tradesmen, walking dog
- do a little light gardening when required (watering plants, picking fruit and vegetables)
  - prepare evening meal and leave to be reheated on employer's return from work
  - occasional evening work when employer entertains, for which overtime will be paid.

work herself; you cannot expect her to be patient, caring and good company for your children at all times if you are asking her to work a 12- or 15-hour day every day. If the hours you work are consistently long and frequently extend into the evenings, you may need to consider an additional support person to take over from your nanny on a regular basis – to babysit on certain nights of the week, for example.

If your needs are more modest, you can consider the live-out option (but see Chapter 8 for rules governing the employment of overseas workers).

Live-in childcare: advantages

- for suitable person whom children like, this provides the most stable care environment for them
- she is likely to be available for work even if she has a head cold
- your home being hers while she works for you, she is less likely to consider changing her job
- she is always at work on time
- as long as it is agreed from the outset and reflected in her salary, she will be available for evening babysitting and night care
- when your children fall ill they will not have to be got out of bed and driven to a childminder or day nursery – assuming you can find one to take them – in the event that you cannot take time off work
- your children can always come home if they are taken ill at school

Live-in childcare: disadvantages

- parents may have to forgo a degree of privacy if the children's carer is living under their roof
- a live-in nanny expects reasonable private accommodation of her own, such as a granny flat, a bedroom with *en suite* bathroom, or at least a bedroom with television
- well qualified and experienced live-in nannies are often expensive
- some nannies expect the use of a car
- children may grow very attached to the nanny because they spend so much time with her, causing jealous feelings on your part and emotional upheaval for the children when the nanny leaves
- a live-in nanny will expect to be able to entertain her friends in your home. You need to make clear what constitutes

Live-in childcare: advantages
— *continued*

- your children can return to their own home and toys after school each day
- a live-in nanny will seem, to your children, like part of the family, someone with whom they can be themselves

Live-in childcare: disadvantages
— *continued*

'reasonable' hospitality – for example, parties and boyfriends in her room in the evening might be unacceptable, while having friends round for morning coffee is o.k.
- rules about what time she comes in at night may have to be established to prevent disturbance to the rest of the family. If she has her own granny flat or lives in your basement and has her own front-door key, this may not be a problem (unless she stays out very late and it affects her work the next day).

Live-out childcare: advantages

- you and your family have the house to yourselves when the nanny leaves in the evening
- you will not have to provide accommodation
- if she is local, your children will benefit from her local contacts and knowledge and she may know some of the mothers at the local mother-and-toddler groups, while a live-in nanny unfamiliar with the area could feel rather isolated
- if she is local you could easily call on her in an out-of-hours emergency

Live-out childcare: disadvantages

- she may not always arrive on time in the morning
- she may take sick leave for a fairly minor illness such as a cold
- she may not be available for evening babysitting
- she will almost certainly not be available to take care of your baby during the night
- she may be less flexible about hours than a live-in nanny. If your own working hours are unpredictable, check the after-hours commitments of any potential live-out nanny beforehand

**Live-out childcare: advantages
— *continued***

- she may have use of her own car while you just contribute to the petrol/mileage
- if you have only one child and your live-out nanny is shared with another family, your child will benefit from the 'extended family' and have other children to play with
- a nanny who lives in her own home is more likely to stay in the area, particularly if she has financial and family ties there, and will probably change jobs less frequently than some of the more independent and career-minded live-in nannies.

**Live-out childcare: disadvantages
— *continued***

- if you are sharing your live-out nanny with another family, the risk of disagreements or other factors jeopardising the arrangement increases. Job requirements must be discussed fully at the outset by the two families and the nanny. The two families must also agree on how they want their children fed, disciplined, educated, entertained and so on.

Cost of childcare

Salary and benefits

Your nanny, whether live-in or live-out, will expect a basic net salary of £100–£300 per week, depending upon where you live in the UK and where your nanny was trained. What she will ask for and what you will pay are a matter of negotiation between the two of you based on how many children you are asking her to look after, what hours you are expecting her to work, and what household duties and additional responsibilities you expect her to undertake. In addition to the nanny's net salary – i.e. the amount that she gets in hand each week – you will have to pay her tax and National Insurance contribution through a pay-as-you-earn (PAYE) scheme, as well as an employer's NI contribution. If she is your sole employee you can deal with the Inland Revenue under the Simplified Deduction Scheme. The employer's control section of your local tax office will be able to advise you. Below is an example of what your total outgoings might be.

Employing a nanny: what it might cost the employer

Salary	£250.00 (per week)
Tax	£36.45 (deducted by employer from gross salary and paid to Inland Revenue)
NI	£19.88 (deducted by employer and paid to Contributions Agency)
Net salary	£193.97 (paid to nanny each week)
Employer's NI	£25.00 (paid by employer to Contributions Agency)
Total	£275.00 (to be found by employer each week)

You may choose to provide your nanny with other benefits such as a car solely for her use, and to cover the cost of its insurance, petrol and maintenance. Some employers pay private health insurance for their nannies and others pay towards a pension scheme. These types of benefit are an individual choice for each employer, but bear in mind that if the nanny you wish to engage received such benefits from her previous employer she is unlikely to want to work for someone who is not prepared to continue them.

Other items to factor into the overall cost of employing a nanny, particularly a live-in one, are higher heating and electricity costs, increased food bills, and additional use of the telephone: many an employer/nanny relationship has crumbled under the weight of too many phone calls made home to parents in Australia or the long calls to friends.

CASE HISTORY: Caroline

Caroline and her husband, both GPs, have three children. Since the birth of the first child the family has employed a live-in nanny, as well as a woman who comes in to clean and do the family laundry. The nanny has sole responsibility for the children while their parents work. She is also responsible for the children during the night, but she does have every weekend off as Caroline and her husband have always arranged matters so that only one of them is on call for emergency medical needs. They provide the nanny with her own room and bathroom, television and car. They have been fortunate to keep the same nanny for the last 10 years.

They estimate that it costs them about £300 per week to pay the nanny's salary, tax, NI and car expenses.

Self-employed childcare

The Inland Revenue permits self-employed status only to child-minders, maternity nurses and temporary nannies. Any other nanny comes within the PAYE system, even if she is shared between two or more families – in which case the administration of her NI and tax can become rather complicated. The Inland Revenue produces a leaflet (IR115) which explains the options. It will also supply tax tables and deduction sheets.

If you do hire a temporary nanny, childminder or maternity nurse who is self-employed, even though it is not your responsibility to ensure that she keeps a decent set of accounts, you should insist on her presenting you with a proper invoice before you hand over a cheque. Then your tax records will be straight.

Nanny payroll services

Many people find it useful to relieve themselves of the burden of dealing with National Insurance and tax calculations by employing one of the nanny payroll services that have sprung up in recent years. There are a handful of such companies in the UK and, for an annual fee per nanny of £100–£200 plus VAT, they will provide a payroll service to employers which includes supplying payslips and P60 forms, updating tax codes and filling in annual returns. They will keep complete payroll records and issue a P45 when a nanny leaves your employment.

Note that, under the current system, failure to file returns by the due date results in a penalty of £100 for each month's delay, plus charges on any liabilities not met.

Au pairs and overseas workers

The employment of au pairs and other overseas workers is regulated by law. Au pairs may work only a certain number of hours a week and should be given their own room, board and an allowance of £30–£40 per week. Any other benefits you wish to give your au pair, such as paying for her to go to college, learning to drive, going home to visit her family or paying for her to go on holiday with your family, are entirely up to you. Au pairs generally do not possess childcare qualifications and should not have unsupervised care of children.

As the rules governing the employment of overseas workers are complex, and subject to government review, the issues are covered in more detail in Chapter 8.

CASE HISTORY: Martin and Patricia

Martin and Patricia have four children between the ages of four and 14. Patricia is an artists' agent who works primarily from home but often attends meetings elsewhere. The family decided to find an au pair through an agency that had supplied satisfactory au pairs for their friends. After one bad experience with the first au pair they were found, they now have Marta, who is 18. Marta's visa states that she must not work more than five hours a day and that she cannot stay in the UK for longer than two years. In return for her work, which includes some light domestic chores, she receives board and lodging and an allowance of £35 per week. She also has two full days a week off, one of which she spends at college studying for a childcare qualification, which is paid for by her employers.

Marta gets the children ready for school/playgroup in the mornings, collects the 4-year-old at lunchtimes and occupies her during the after-noons. Patricia takes over when the older children come home from school, unless she has a late meeting outside. This arrangement is expected to continue until the youngest child starts full-time schooling, by which time Marta's visa will have expired.

Children with special needs

If one of your children is disabled or has special needs, your local Social Services or health authority will be able to provide assistance and advice on childcare arrangements. FRES and the Professional Association of Nursery Nurses are other good sources of advice, and should be able to help you find private agencies that can provide staff with nursing qualifications as well as trained nannies.

As the circumstances of children with disabilities and special needs are so individual and vary so much, it has not been possible to include reference to them in the general checklists in this chapter.

If you are the parent of a special-needs child you should be look-ing for a carer or nanny who has qualifications, training and experi-ence relevant to your circumstances. The more advanced childcare qualifications cover the subject of children with special needs, but there is no substitute for experience: if you can find someone who has had some experience in caring for children with a variety of dis-abilities this will be more valuable than any diploma. Depending upon the complexity of your child's needs it may be that you need to advertise for a carer or apply to an agency that handles nurses rather than nannies. FRES has a nurses/carers section and can sup-ply a list of relevant member agencies.

The childcare situation becomes more difficult (and, unfortu-nately, more expensive) if you have one special-needs child and other children who require ordinary supervisory care. You will then need to find someone who is skilled in both types of childcare or employ more than one person – for example, by splitting your childcare between a live-in nanny and a childminder.

Babysitters

Babysitting is another area where too many people tend to go for the cheap option rather than fully thinking through the risks of leaving, say, a 14-year-old (the legal minimum age allowed for a babysitter) in charge of pre-school children at night. No matter how sensible your friend's teenage daughter may seem, she may not have the maturity and experience to deal with an emergency such as the sudden, severe illness of an infant or a fire in the house. In addition, you should be employing someone to babysit who can drive, as she may need to whisk your child off to the local hospital in the event of an accident.

Most people use babysitters that they know, such as friends or rel-atives, but if you decide to recruit through an agency you should fol-low the guidelines given in this book for hiring agency childcare. The babysitter should have been thoroughly vetted by the agency, and he or she should have relevant experience, possibly a childcare qualifica-tion, a knowledge of first aid, and the ability to speak good English.

You should always leave a contact phone number with the babysitter when you go out, or, if that is not possible, ring in every so often to check that everything is as it should be. The babysitter should not use your telephone, except in emergency, as it should be kept free for you to ring in whenever you wish. You should leave written instructions about care of the children and prepare beforehand feeds for babies, other special meals etc.

Experienced babysitters, whether a friend or through an agency, charge £2.50–£5 an hour.

CHILDCARE CHECKLIST	YES	NO	SOMETIMES
Would your carer need to:			
start work at 7 a.m.?			
get children up?			
prepare breakfast?			
dress children?			
take children to school?			
take children to playgroup?			
look after pre-school children at home?			
prepare lunch?			
do children's laundry?			
do light housework?			
take children out to playgrounds/for walks etc.?			
take children to daytime appointments?			
collect child from school if one falls ill?			
call in the doctor at home?			
collect children from school?			
take children to extra lessons/parties/clubs etc.?			
prepare tea?			
supervise homework?			
supervise television-watching and play?			
stay with children until parent comes home?			
bathe infants and supervise older children's bathtime?			
prepare them for bed?			
babysit some evenings?			
assist children during the night?			
look after children when they are ill?			

CASE HISTORY: David

David, a widower with two school-age children, has used the services of a childminder, a live-out housekeeper and a babysitter since his wife died so that he can keep on working full-time. David drops off his children at the childminder's house each day at 8 a.m. She gives them breakfast and takes them to school. Every afternoon she collects them, feeds them, and supervises their homework and television-viewing until their father picks them up at 6 p.m. David and the childminder have agreed that she will also be available to collect them if they should become ill or have an accident at school. David has given a signed letter to this effect to the headmistress at the children's school. David pays the childminder £2.50 per hour; as she is self-employed she is responsible for her own tax and NI.

His housekeeper comes in three afternoons a week and does the cleaning, washing, ironing and cooking. David also employs a regular babysitter when he needs to go out in the evening or, occasionally, works on a Saturday. Both the babysitter and the housekeeper are paid £3 per hour. In all, in a typical week, David pays about £100 for domestic help.

Assessing care for the elderly

Most elderly people in need of care, or their carers, contact Social Services initially for an assessment of their care needs. Social workers, who have responsibility for the elderly in the community, have a great deal of experience in assessing needs and can make sure that nothing is overlooked. Unfortunately, local authorities have had to cut back on services to such an extent that some Social Services departments are either turning down applications for assessment or the waiting list is extremely long. It should also be noted that having an assessment done does not guarantee that the local Social Services department will be able to provide or arrange for the services that you or the person you care for need.

By law, Social Services departments must carry out a care assessment in the following circumstances:

- if someone appears to the local authority to be in need of a community care service (NHS and Community Care Act 1990, section 47)

- if someone is disabled (NHS and Community Care Act 1990, section 47, and Disabled Persons [Services, Representation and Consultation] Act 1986, section 4)
- if one person is helping to look after another (Disabled Persons [Services, Representation and Consultation] Act 1986, sections 4 and 8, and Carers [Recognition and Services] Act 1995, section 1).

In practice, some local authorities will refuse to carry out an assessment if they consider, after a preliminary telephone conversation, that you or the person you look after do not qualify for help. If you are met with a refusal and you want to challenge it, you can contact Age Concern England's Information Line★ during working hours, Monday to Friday, to ask for advice.

Most private care agencies offer free assessments, but these companies are, of course, commercially motivated and you will need to make sure that you are not being assessed as being in need of rather more help than you in fact require. Ask two or three agencies to carry out an independent assessment of your needs before deciding which one to use. An alternative is to employ a private consultant who is paid a fee for assessing a home care situation and whose job it is to provide a care plan. Armed with this plan, you can then shop around.

The level of assessment carried out by Social Services varies from the 'low-level' to 'comprehensive'. For example, based on the initial telephone contact, a 'low-level' assessment may be carried out, because Social Services anticipates that your needs are simple, such as installing special equipment in your home to make certain tasks easier, or a once-weekly cleaning service. For someone whose care needs are greater, a 'comprehensive' assessment is carried out, which may involve professionals from other areas of community care, such as a district nurse, physiotherapist, doctor or occupational therapist.

The assessment process, in effect, is in three parts:

- the individual's capabilities, care needs and home environment
- the services that are available locally (either through Social Services or through private or voluntary agencies) to meet that individual's needs
- the applicant's finances.

Participating in the assessment process

To get the best possible help available it is essential that the person in need of support, and anyone who currently gives a level of support to that person, is involved in the assessment process. Honesty is essential – pride has to be set aside. No one, whatever their age, finds it easy to admit that they need help getting on and off the toilet or that they can no longer prepare their own food. A social worker is there not to pass judgement on an individual but to see what help can be offered and whether that person will accept that help.

Make a list of tasks that you can do, tasks that you are having problems doing now and tasks that you have been unable to do for some time. You may be recovering from an illness or hospitalisation which has reduced your capabilities for the time being but they may be much improved in six months' time. An assessor can look at all these factors, match up the current needs with the current services available, and monitor the situation for the future.

The list should be comprehensive, including everything from special dietary needs and physical limitations to your emotional, religious and cultural needs. There is no point in stating that you cannot prepare your own meals then, when the social worker has arranged meals on wheels, telling her that you only eat kosher food. By the same token, an elderly Asian woman may find it extremely distressing to be bathed by anyone other than a woman of her own race, while an elderly man may wish to be attended by male care workers only. Everyone has the right to maintain personal dignity whether asking for state or private help.

Be honest about physical problems such as incontinence or fainting spells. The severity of your medical problems determines what level of experience or training your carers have to have in order to assist you in your home.

You must also be forthright about your emotional needs. If you need your privacy and cannot bear the thought of someone else sleeping in your house at night, you have the right to explore other options. You may be able to have a carer come in first thing in the morning to get you out of bed and last thing at night to put you into bed. Night-time cover in case of illness could be provided by wearing a personal alarm that is linked up to an emergency call-out service.

Do not omit small details like being unable to put on a pair of stockings or go shopping because you can no longer read print.

An assessment, whether carried out by Social Services or privately, should be written down and summarised, then shown to the individual in need. A local authority complaints procedure can be followed if the assessment is felt to be inadequate, biased or unhelpful. You can also ask to be re-assessed if you are unhappy with the outcome. If you accept a care package and subsequently find that it does not meet your needs you can also ask for a re-assessment, although most local authorities undertake regular assessments of care packages as a matter of course. If you are unhappy with a private agency's assessment, take your business to another agency.

Using an independent care adviser

The number of independent care advisers has grown steadily over recent years. Members of the Association of Independent Care Advisers (AICA),* formed in 1994, offer advice on care, care management and monitoring. Independent care advisers operate in two ways: some offer free care assessments, while others charge a consultancy fee. All care advisers adhere to the AICA's code of practice, which states that they must be truly independent and not favour any care provider over another. Nevertheless, some do offer free care assessments and receive a commission from the care providers they recommend. You are, however, under no obligation to use the services of the care providers the adviser recommends. Other AICA members offer a consultancy service, for which they charge the client a fee. This is typically £50–£75 per hour, and an assessment of care needs will generally take a minimum of two hours.

The AICA states in its code of practice:

> The independent status of members is of key importance. Membership is not permitted to individuals or organisations with a financial or commercial interest in domiciliary or residential care services.
>
> Members are entitled to receive payments from any body or organisation in return for the introduction of clients. Members may not, however, compromise their independence by entering into agreements to fill a minimum number of vacancies or deliver a particular volume of business.

The AICA says that its members have a wealth of specialised knowledge, not just about what services exist locally but also on topics such as statutory allowances and methods of claiming. In addition, the independent care adviser can help the family or individual negotiate with Social Services, using his or her knowledge of the system to save the client time and frustration.

CASE HISTORY: William

William's elderly father, who lives on his own nearby, has a care package arranged through his local Social Services department. Most of the care was provided by a private agency contracted by the department. On three occasions agency staff left, giving little or no notice, and the agency took at least a week to replace them. This caused great inconvenience to William and his father, with William having to take time off work each time to provide emergency cover. They complained to Social Services after the second occasion, and Social Services took the matter up with the care provider, which reassured the department it would not happen again. When it happened for the third time Social Services withdrew the contract from that agency and another company was contracted to provide emergency cover.

The cost of care in your home

Despite the importance of the work, care workers are surprisingly low paid. The Greater Manchester Low Pay Unit issues pay factsheets from time to time which give workers some idea of average rates of pay in their chosen occupation. Otherwise, any local authority will tell you the average rate of pay for their care workers, which will give you a yardstick for when you are making arrangements yourself. Minimim wage legislation is likely to have an effect at the lower end of the scale in due course.

If you are in receipt of state benefits and will receive subsidised care services through your local Social Services department you can expect to pay £10–£20 per week for those services on average. Weekly payments as low as £3 have been recorded and some as high as £40.

A private care assistant – one whom you engage yourself rather than through an agency – who has gained experience of the field through working for a local authority will expect at least the local authority manual worker rates shown above. Rates of pay for services through private agencies are considerably higher and probably reflect the true cost of such a labour-intensive and demanding industry.

NEEDS CHECKLIST: PHYSICAL TASKS	YES	NO	NOT AT THE MOMENT (temporary situation such as after discharge from hospital)
Can you do the following:			
get out of bed in the morning?			
get to the toilet in the night?			
get to the bathroom and wash yourself?			
bathe or shower unaided?			
dress yourself?			
put on socks, stockings or tights?			
reach light switches or alarms?			
hear the telephone, doorbell, radio and television?			
read print?			
plug in a vacuum cleaner and use it?			
hold a duster and use it?			
make your bed or change your bed?			
do your laundry?			
stand or sit and use an iron?			
see clearly to give yourself the correct prescribed medication?			
open cans or packets?			
hold a saucepan?			
prepare a meal?			
wash up dishes?			
go out to the local shops?			
make yourself a cup of tea?			
get up your stairs?			

NEEDS CHECKLIST: PHYSICAL TASKS – *continued*	YES	NO	NOT AT THE MOMENT (temporary situation such as after discharge from hospital)
Does someone look after you:			
all the time?			
some of the time?			
Are you alone?			
Is there someone on hand if there is an emergency, e.g. a warden (a neighbour may not always be there)?			
Do you have a personal alarm?			
Do you need regular medical services, e.g. chiropodist, district nurse, physiotherapist, speech therapist?			
Are you incontinent?			
Do you have any other medical problems such as diabetes, fits, dizzy spells?			
Do you have a speech problem?			
Are you recovering from an illness or an operation?			

Assessing the need for domestic help

Perhaps the most important factor when you are employing someone in your home, over and above whether or not they can do the job properly, is security. The risks are enormous, yet all too few people think about this when they hand over a front-door key to the daily cleaner, jobbing gardener or cook who comes in the afternoon to prepare the dinner party.

Although you cannot run a police check on every cleaner who comes in for three hours a week, taking up references and making a few discreet enquiries locally should establish whether the person

59

in question is trustworthy. More and more busy people are employing domestic staff whom they never see but to whom they give unlimited access to their home. The need to improve security is one reason why busy Americans have turned to 'domestic out-sourcing consultants' (see Chapter 2): these people check out the backgrounds of domestic staff, communicate with them on a regular basis and monitor the standard of their work.

While the emotional considerations associated with the welfare of children or elderly people may not apply, the distress that can be caused by the theft or breakage of treasured possessions – or for that matter the annoyance of petty theft that is hard to prove – should not be underestimated.

Employing and keeping domestic staff requires as much attention to the job description as employing a nanny or carer. The first assessment to make about your domestic help needs is whether or not the housework is to be 'light'. Be realistic: if you have four cats and three children, the cleaning tasks are not going to be 'light'. If, on the other hand, you live on your own or with a partner, you are both out at work all day and you tend to eat out in restaurants, the housework will consist of dusting, vacuuming, washing up breakfast dishes and making beds – which can certainly be classed as 'light' housework.

If you are in a position to employ full-time live-in staff, an agency should be able to carry out a comprehensive assessment of your requirements free of charge. An agency's experience of domestic service and what is on offer is valuable. It will tell you, for example, what a modern cook/housekeeper expects her duties to be, such as whether she expects to be supported by a cleaner, or whether the size of your home means that she will probably manage the cleaning herself. An agency will assess whether your demands on the time of a chauffeur mean that you cannot reasonably expect him to be a handyman as well, or it may tell you that the chauffeur/handyman is in short supply at present and your chances of getting someone who can combine the two jobs are remote.

The checklist below is aimed at the majority of people employing domestic staff who use a variety of sources through which to find them.

DOMESTIC REQUIREMENTS	YES	NO	SOMETIMES
Cleaning			
Vacuum the carpets throughout every day			
Vacuum once a week			
Vacuum carpets in living areas every day and bedrooms once or twice a week			
Dust throughout once or twice a week			
Polish wood once a week			
Clean bathroom every day			
Clean kitchen sink and surfaces every day			
Put bleach down sinks and toilets every day			
Wash kitchen floor at least once a week			
Clean oven once a week			
Beat rugs out once a week			
Wash light fittings and damp-clean pictures once a week			
Wash front porch and doorstep once a week			
Clean conservatory when needed			
Wash windows inside once a week			
Change cushion covers and curtains when needed			
Vacuum upholstery once a week			
Laundry			
Load washing machine every day			
Wash delicate items by hand			
Strip beds once a week and wash bedding			
Take dry-cleaning to shop or organise collection			

DOMESTIC REQUIREMENTS	YES	NO	SOMETIMES
Laundry — *continued*			
Deal with collection of laundry by laundry service			
Hang washing out to dry or tumble-dry			
Iron clothes			
Put laundered clothes and linen away			
Deal with incontinence laundry			
Wash dirty nappies			
Wash pets' bedding			
Other chores			
Make beds every day			
Change beds once a week, or more frequently if there are special needs			
Supervise children			
Feed children			
Feed pets			
Take dogs for a walk			
Let cats out			
Domestic chores			
Prepare meals singly			
Prepare meals for several days and freeze			
Do shopping			
Do banking			
Pay for other services, e.g. window-cleaner and gardener			
Collect pension			
Provide transport and escort to appointments			
Gardening			
Mow lawn			

DOMESTIC REQUIREMENTS	YES	NO	SOMETIMES
Gardening — *continued*			
Weed flower beds			
Seasonal planting			
Plant and maintain vegetable and fruit crops			
Maintain greenhouse			
Provide cut flowers for the house			
Look after house plants			
Plant and maintain hanging baskets and tubs			
Prune and spray trees			
Clear leaves in autumn			
Maintain compost heap			
Build and supervise bonfires of garden waste			
Water garden in summer			
Maintain sprinkler system			
Aerate and fertilise lawn			
Maintain garden tools			
Creosote garden shed every year			
Sterilise and clean greenhouse every year			
Do special jobs e.g. build a patio/ pergola/garden furniture			
Maintain garden pond and look after fish			
General			
Full-time chauffeuring			
Occasional chauffeuring			
Maintain employer's car (clean, fill up with petrol, oil and water etc.)			
Organise maintenance of employer's car			
Do repairs around the house			

DOMESTIC REQUIREMENTS	YES	NO	SOMETIMES
General — *continued*			
Organise major repairs or building work			
Maintain swimming-pool			
House-sit while employer is away			
Pet-sit while employer is away			
Shop and prepare food for parties and dinner parties			
Clear up and wash dishes after parties			
Buy and arrange flowers throughout the house			
Provide companionship			
Provide secretarial assistance (dealing with mail, answering phone etc.)			
Cook on a full-time basis			
Prepare a selection of menus each week			
Deal with special dietary needs			
Buy and maintain food stocks in the house (including snacks and drinks)			
Lay and light open fires in the house			

The list of domestic chores that an individual or household may require is endless, and you will no doubt wish to add your own items to those provided on the checklists here.

Once you have completed the list of the tasks you want done, the next step is to write down any particular preferences you have in terms of *how* they are done. For example, how do you like your beds to be made: hospital corners, fitted sheets, duvet over the top of a tucked-in sheet etc.? Rather than complaining after your domestic help has made the bed in his or her own way, explain from the outset how you would like it done. That way, you can prevent the relationship from degenerating into one of mutual grumbling.

Preparation of food is an area where most people have strong likes and dislikes, not just about the choice of food but about how it is prepared. Some people like vegetables to be lightly steamed, others like them boiled to a mush. Some people like their steak very rare, others like it incinerated, and so on. Specify your preferences in advance.

Cleaning is another potential source of dispute, particularly if you have antique furniture that needs special treatment when cleaned and polished, or valuable Persian rugs that should not be vacuumed every day. Make sure such points are noted.

The cost of domestic help

Live-in staff are very expensive to maintain and, if your standards are particularly high, you are likely to pay a premium to acquire the quality of staff to meet your expectations.

Local live-out staff will be much cheaper because you can tailor their hours to suit your budget. You will need to decide what tasks are essential for them to complete during the hours you employ them, and what tasks you can cope with yourself. You may decide to do all your own washing and give the domestic help the ironing. Or you may decide to do the creative work in the garden yourself and ask the gardener to do the heavier work. Expect to pay £3–£5 an hour for local live-out domestic staff that you hire yourself, and £5–£10 an hour for staff employed through an agency. Gardeners charge about £10 an hour or a fee for each special job.

Ironing service firms charge £5 per hour on average, but collection and delivery may be extra. Laundry services usually charge per item or per weight of dry clothing. This varies according to where you live but the range is as follows: washing £3–£5 plus cost of washers and dryers to have laundry 'service washed' at a laundrette; full laundry service (washing, drying and ironing) £2–£4 per shirt, £1.50–£3.50 per pair of trousers or jeans, £2–£4 per dry weight of other laundry; ironing only 60p–£2 per shirt, 80p–£2 per pair of trousers or jeans, £1–£2 per dry weight of other laundry. Collection and delivery charges are extra: most companies quote free collection and delivery if the total bill is more than £10–£15; otherwise, the charge is between £1 and £2.50. Washing dropped off at a local laundrette to be service washed can usually be picked up later the same day. Full laundry services are usually a minimum 48-hour turnaround. If you deliver ironing yourself to a local company, turnaround is usually 24 hours. If ironing is collected and delivered, it is usually a minimum of 48 hours.

Caterers generally charge so much per head for parties and a lump sum for preparation of a dinner party. The service offered by caterers will cost more if you want them to serve at table and clear up afterwards. The cost of catering services in your home will depend upon your choice of food and drink and can vary from £5 per head (for a very basic meal or, say, a children's party) to £50 per head (the best champagne and equivalent food). Many catering companies have a minimum charge and it is not economical to use them unless you are hosting a dinner party for at least eight people. The larger companies will not consider catering for fewer than 50 people. It is often the extras that push the price up. For example, a marquee erected in a (large) garden for a special anniversary celebration can add about £1,000 to the price.

CASE HISTORY: Janet

Janet, a divorced mother of two school-age children, works as a receptionist, sharing a job with another woman. Her hours are 9 a.m. until 1 p.m., five days a week, so she is able to drop off her children at school, go to work and do some housework in the afternoon before picking up her children. As well as her salary she receives generous maintenance from her ex-husband and child benefit, so she can afford to pay £20 a week for someone to come in and do her ironing for her. She also pays someone to mow the lawn and do any heavy work in the garden once a week. This costs her about £15 on average.

Tax and National Insurance contributions

If you pay an individual employee more than the Lower Earnings Limit (£64 per week in 1998, rising to £80 in 1999) you have to pay his or her National Insurance contributions. The employer's contribution per week (as of 1998) is as follows:

Employee's weekly wage	Employer's NI contribution
£64–£110	3%
£110–£155	5%
£155–£210	7%
£210 and over	10%

NI contributions must also be paid for overseas workers. However, if you pay your cleaner £30 per week and he/she earns a similar amount working for several other households, thereby taking her above the Lower Earnings Limit, it is not your responsibility to pay National Insurance contributions. Similarly, if you employ someone or several people on a contract through an agency, and the agency retains responsibility for its staff, the agency will deal with all tax and NI matters. Nor do you have to pay tax or NI when you employ a freelance person or small business to undertake jobs such as window-cleaning, catering or indeed any service supplied on a contract basis.

If you are intending to employ someone full-time, whether live-in or not, tax and NI will have to be built into your budget. Once you have calculated the cost of employing someone directly, including tax and NI, you can check whether it would be more cost-effective to employ someone through an agency (if you are meeting all of the cost yourself, rather than receiving state help). You may find that the costs work out about the same, as the agencies will have built into their charges all tax and NI, but using an agency will alleviate some of the burden of recruitment and administration.

Chapter 4

Advertising and using an agency

If you decide to find your domestic help yourself through an advertisement, whether it is a card in the local post office or an advertisement in a publication such as *The Lady*, be as specific as possible about what the job entails. That way you will cut out time-wasting on both your part and the applicants'. If you want someone to do the laundry and ironing and feed your pets as well as clean the house, say so in your advertisement, rather than advertising simply for a 'cleaner'. By so doing, you know that everyone who applies for the job is willing to undertake all of the tasks involved.

Similarly, if you want someone to dig over your entire garden, move paving slabs and haul out old tree stumps, make sure you specify this rather than advertising simply for a 'gardener'. Otherwise, you will receive applications from all local gardeners looking for work, including elderly ones who are keen and experienced but unable to cope with the heavy work involved.

Part-time housekeeper wanted

To do all household cleaning, laundry and ironing for family of four, and prepare some midday meals, four mornings a week. Must like dogs and children. Must have a sense of humour. Payment by negotiation.

References required. Ring [tel. no.] for an appointment.

Live-out nanny wanted for two small children aged 18 months and 4 years. Hours 8.30 a.m.–5 p.m. Use of car provided. No housework required. Only NNEB-qualified applicants need apply.

Good rate of pay. References required.

Ring [tel. no.] for an appointment.

Jobbing gardener wanted to cope with very large, mature garden. Duties include mowing the lawn, weeding, maintaining the vegetable bed and fruit cage, putting in bedding plants and pruning trees. Garden equipment provided. Probably enough work for two full days a week. Rate by negotiation. References required.

Ring [tel. no.] for an appointment.

Security considerations

If you live alone, do not, under any circumstances, mention that fact in an advertisement or on the telephone. Indeed, if you are advertising in a publication, it is a good idea not to give a telephone number at all but to use a box number (see below). When you interview someone, ask a friend or relative to be in the house with you. If you are confident that the person you are interviewing is trustworthy, because he or she is already known to you, has been recommended by someone you know or has good references which you have checked, you can explain that you live alone. An elderly person living alone and looking for care assistance or domestic help should interview only people who have been personally recommended; alternatively, use a reputable agency.

Other details about the job that for security reasons should not be mentioned in the advertisement include a requirement for the person to handle money, perhaps to pay tradesmen, shop, collect your pension or do banking for you. Make a list of any extra tasks to refer to during an interview, but not on the telephone.

Advertising in a publication

Most national and local newspapers and magazines will sell you advertising space in their pages. Looking at the advertisements in the magazines or local papers you are considering will help you to decide which publication is most likely to reach the type of applicant you want to attract. The publication itself can of course accept no responsibility for the quality – or lack – of response that your advertisement elicits: it is your responsibility to make your advertisement sufficiently attractive to the reader and to state within it what type of qualifications/experience you require.

You are expected to honour the Advertising Standards Authority★ Code of Practice in that advertisements should be 'legal, decent, honest and truthful'. Do not make extravagant promises in your advertisement, such as 'whatever your present salary is we will double it!'. As well as contravening the Code, misrepresenting the job will result in your spending hours in fruitless interviews with applicants who make it clear that they are not interested because the job is very different from what they expected.

Using a box number

If you are advertising in a national magazine, or a magazine like *The Lady* which is read all over the world, using a box number has several advantages over giving your telephone number. First, it protects you from receiving unwanted calls from disturbed people who pick your phone number at random from the magazine. Second, if you are advertising for full-time professional staff and the wording indicates that yours is a wealthy family, potential burglars have the benefit of a phone number to check whether or not you are at home. Third, it saves you time and inconvenience. Answering hundreds of telephone calls from applicants, most of whom may be unsuitable, is a wearisome task. If you ask the magazine to give you a box number, all of the applicants will write to the magazine and the magazine will forward the mail to you. That way, you can sift through all the letters and choose a short list in peace and quiet, without the phone continually ringing. You can then contact the applicants that interest you and organise the interviews.

Magazines and newspapers that offer a box reply service do, however, suggest that you mention the general location of the job in the advertisement in order not to waste the applicant's time. 'Nanny wanted in remote but lovely Cotswold village' tells the would-be nanny exactly what she needs to know, without compromising your home security. Depending on the publication you choose, a box number will cost you £7–£20 per insertion of the advertisement.

Local newspapers

Local newspapers are a good place to advertise if your domestic help needs are modest and you want live-out help to come to your house on a regular basis, which means that they need to live locally. They are not a good place to advertise for childcare. Qualified nannies will not be scanning the classified advertisements of local papers for a new position: they will be looking at the publications that have an established track record of advertising childcare positions.

Local papers will generally provide you with a box number, although most people advertising in local publications include their telephone numbers. This still leaves you open to nuisance calls, even if the worst is a great many calls from firms selling double-glazing.

Specialist publications

In addition to *The Lady*, which is long established as a vehicle for communicating domestic vacancies and situations wanted, specialist publications, such as *Nursery World* and *Professional Nanny*, and magazines which cater to the senior citizens market, such as *Choice*,* are alternatives to consider. Details of relevant publications appear in the 'Addresses and further reading' section in this guide.

Some newspapers occasionally run special features on childcare or eldercare and agencies might advertise in that feature, though not individuals. Most of the broadsheet newspapers, such as *The Times*, *The Daily Telegraph* and *The Guardian*, accept advertisements from individuals seeking or offering domestic situations. The price varies according to the size of your advertisement and whether it is a 'classified' (unboxed lines of type) or a 'display' advertisement (with a box or border around the text to make the advertisement more eye-catching). The price will also vary according to the circulation of the publication.

When you select a publication for your advertisement consider whether you may be spreading your net too wide and be likely to attract a huge response but not necessarily of the quality you seek. It is surprising how many people respond to advertisements that plainly ask for certain qualifications or a minimum number of years' experience even though they do not meet the criteria. Rather than advertising in a national publication, a better option might be to contact the relevant professional body (see 'Addresses and further reading') and enquire whether it has its own publication in which you could advertise. You know then that your advertisement will be seen by the most appropriate readership.

CASE HISTORY: Petra and Michael

Petra and Michael have two children, who attend private day schools, and live in London. Michael is an investment banker, Petra a design consultant. They have a substantial joint income. They employ a husband-and-wife team from Poland who between them act as chauffeur, housekeeper, nanny, cook and handyman. This couple lives in a large flat in the mews at the back of the main house. Petra originally placed an advertisement in *The Lady* and received more than 50 applications from couples, who all seemed very experienced. Only four of the couples were English and about half of the applications were from couples that Petra considered too old to manage such a large house and two fairly boisterous children. They chose Agnieska and Jan for their quiet but confident personalities and the fact that Jan had been a driver in the Army. Agnieska turned out to be an excellent cook and the arrangement has worked extremely well. Petra and Michael pay the couple a joint salary of £300 per week in addition to their board and lodging. They also pay for private health insurance for the couple and contribute towards a pension scheme for them. Petra admits that they are probably generous compared with some employers, but are aware of the risk of the couple being poached.

Advertising costs

Advertising rates vary from publication to publication and will depend on the type of advertisement, number of words used, and so on, but examples of rates (including VAT) are as follows. To advertise for a nanny in *TNT Magazine* (read by Australasians in the UK), approximately £50; in *The Lady* (read by professional nannies, as well as other professional domestic staff), about £60; in *Nursery*

World (read by professional nannies and trained childcarers), about £30; in a local newspaper, approximately £20.

Advertising locally

For modest domestic help requirements you could advertise locally, with a card in the local shop or post office. In this situation you will have to include your phone number, but you can reduce the inconvenience involved by stating the preferred hours for an applicant to ring. For example:

Cleaner wanted

Two hours a day, five days a week, to clean for a household of three fairly tidy adults. Good hourly rates. Please ring [tel. no.] between 4 p.m. and 6 p.m. ONLY.

College noticeboards and newsletters

If you are seeking to fill a position that requires qualifications, such as a cook, nanny or butler, you could try advertising through the relevant colleges, either the specialist colleges listed in the back of this book or local colleges that run courses appropriate to your requirements. Most colleges have a communications network that enables them to help students get work. This is either highly organised, such as the college running its own agency, or something as basic as a noticeboard in the corridor.

Recruiting through an agency

Finding agencies in your local area presents no difficulties: *Yellow Pages* and *Thomson* directories will contain lists. Finding a *good* agency, however, requires more research. A friend's positive experience of using a particular agency is the most valuable recommendation, but if you are unable to source any personal recommendations you must ensure that the agency at least belongs to a trade organisation and adheres to a code of practice.

FRES has almost 4,000 agencies among its membership. These include domestic staff, general recruitment, and nurses and carers agencies. FRES states that all of its members:

- commit to a code of practice aimed at ensuring best practice in recruitment
- undergo a stringent vetting procedure
- must be granted a certificate every year to confirm that they adhere to FRES standards
- are subject to arbitration, complaints and disciplinary procedures
- are recognised as demonstrating approved standards in recruitment.

FRES's arbitration, complaints and disciplinary procedures help to ensure that any agency found to be inadequate or negligent is subject to a penalty, and means that you have a central body to complain to if something goes wrong. Always choose an agency that belongs to a reputable umbrella organisation, and check that the agency managers hold suitable qualifications, such as membership of the Institute of Employment Consultants.★

CASE HISTORY: Ellen

A divorced mother of three children who works full-time as a senior nursing officer in a large hospital in the north of England, Ellen used an agency to find a live-in housekeeper who could look after the children and the house while she worked the more lucrative night shift at her hospital. Being anxious to find the right person and bearing the safety and welfare of her children uppermost in her mind, she insisted that any shortlisted applicants must be registered childminders who were (accordingly) suitably experienced and had been, at one time, approved by Social Services. She interviewed eight shortlisted applicants but did not warm to any of their personalities, so asked the agency to try again. It was able to send her another five applicants. She liked one middle-aged woman in particular, as did the children, so with the agreement of the agency and the applicant the housekeeper started work on a three-month trial basis. Fortunately this worked well and the housekeeper has now been with the family for over a year. Ellen pays her £150 per week (some of which is contributed by Ellen's ex-husband) and the housekeeper has her own room and bathroom and use of Ellen's car during the day.

Nanny agencies

The fact that employment agencies in the UK are not required to hold a licence, nor are those running the agencies required to be qualified in any way (see Chapter 2), is a widespread concern. Indeed, the national press has reported several cases of mothers setting up their own nanny agencies – with the best of motives, but with no professional qualifications whatsoever.

PANN advises nannies to use an agency, for their own protection, particularly if it is their first job as a nanny. In particular, it advises them to use agencies that are registered members of FRES and have qualified staff in charge.

PANN's definition of a good agency is one that:

- does not charge the nanny a registration fee
- is open to questions
- has vacancies in the area where the nanny wishes to work
- has a vetting procedure for prospective employers
- interviews nannies and thoroughly checks their qualifications and references
- assists in negotiating terms and conditions
- assists in drawing up a contract between employer and employee
- offers after-placement support to both employer and employee
- arbitrates in the event of disputes.

Au pair agencies

Another area where the lack of regulation is keenly felt is in the au pair sector. Demand for au pairs has never been higher. As a result, 'agencies' have sprung up all over the UK, including a high proportion that are run by private individuals from their living rooms whose only qualification for setting up the agency is that they have a few friends in France, Germany or Switzerland.

The International Au Pair Association was founded in 1994 during the World Youth Student Travel Conference in Vancouver, Canada. IAPA is still in its infancy, but it already has many full, associate and affiliate members in the UK and throughout the world. Its members are expected to adhere to IAPA guidelines, including those governing the selection of both au pairs and families, and the rights and responsibilities of all parties involved. A good member agency of IAPA will:

- take great care in vetting host families
- ask host families to fill in a form detailing all their requirements
- expect detailed character references from au pairs
- take great care in matching au pairs and host families
- provide full and clear information to both parties at all times
- provide a code of conduct for the au pair and the host family (see Chapter 7)
- make it very clear that au pairs and mothers' helps only *assist* with children, and that only qualified nannies may have unsupervised charge of children
- request and thoroughly check all references for anyone involved in childcare
- provide advice to au pairs and host families on legislation, health insurance, travel etc.
- provide on-going support to the au pair and host family, particularly the former, by introducing her to other au pairs in her area and organising social events or meetings at regular intervals.

CASE HISTORY: Diane and David

Diane and David applied to an agency for an au pair. They wanted an au pair who would be excellent with children, knew enough English to communicate with them and would not mind doing a bit of light housework. A local agency found the 'the perfect au pair': Spanish, 22 years old and the oldest of nine children, Maria loved looking after children and was interested in improving her already excellent English. Diane and David met her at the airport but within three days they discovered that she was not their Maria but a girl called Rosa, although her English was so poor that she answered to the name Maria. She was 18, the youngest of a family of three and very spoiled. She did not like children or housework and came to London to have a good time. Diane demanded the real Maria, but the agency head was away on holiday.

They were stuck with Rosa for three weeks and when the agency head returned and they again demanded Maria, it appeared that she had been sent to another family who, understandably, did not want to part with her. Nothing could be done, including having their £30 fee refunded, because the 'agency' subsequently disappeared. Rosa, meanwhile, found herself a boyfriend and moved out, much to everyone's relief. Diane and David never took the au pair route again.

Domiciliary care agencies

Over 300 nurses-and-carers agencies are members of FRES. The Nurses and Carers section of FRES describes the role of the domiciliary care agency as follows:

> Private care agencies provide a much-valued home care service to the public. Elderly and disabled people are a particularly vulnerable group. It is important that the home care service which they receive is of high quality and one that pays due regard to their safety in their own homes. All this demands that the staff engaged to provide such services are competent, reliable and trustworthy.

FRES offers advice to carers seeking to join an agency and to clients wishing to select an agency. It recommends that carers choosing an agency to join check that the agency:

- supplies the work the carer requires
- offers induction and other training opportunities
- offers an 'on call' service
- is a member of FRES.

Clients choosing an agency should check that the agency:

- provides full details of all charges
- ensures that all carers are adequately trained
- supplies a service appropriate to their requirements
- provides an 'on call' service
- provides carers with accurate information prior to assignment
- is a member of FRES.

An important part of the FRES code of practice concerns agencies assessing the competence and suitability of a carer before taking her on. Any agency providing workers to care for the elderly *must* be able to vouch for their honesty, reliability, competence and experience. This requires the care worker to provide comprehensive information to the agency about employment history and qualifications, in addition to employment and character references, all of which should be checked and double-checked.

The United Kingdom Home Care Association (UKHCA)* is the national representative association for member organisations providing care, including nursing care, to people in their own homes. Its code of practice goes even further than that of FRES in that it instructs its members to make the client's rights the top priority in domiciliary care (see box below).

UKHCA's code of practice

Dignity and value   The dignity and value of every client must be respected.

Personal choice   Home-care organisations must allow each individual to exercise his or her full potential for personal choice of opportunities and lifestyles. The organisation should ensure that the client to be cared for is consulted directly, or by use of an advocate, in decisions over the provision, extent and timing of any care planned, also over the withdrawal of any service. Where, for reasons of mental frailty, the client who is being cared for is not able to participate fully in planning care, consideration should nevertheless be given to his or her wishes, insofar as these are expressed and are practical. Account should also be taken of the needs and rights of carers to lead their lives without unreasonable levels of demands and stress. The rights of clients not to accept in their own homes care workers with whom they are not compatible must be upheld.

Information   Each client has a right to a detailed explanation of the service being offered, including, for example, information about costs and exactly what those costs cover, and information about such matters as whether the organisation will provide a replacement if a care worker is ill or unavailable. Member organisations should take responsibility for ensuring, insofar as they are able, that clients are made aware of other services and sources of help.

The rights of the client are accorded similar importance in the code of practice of AICA, which is comparable to that of UKHCA.

The one thing that all of these organisations fail to recommend in their codes of practice is that, wherever possible, the client should be provided with the same carer for a reasonable length of time in order that he/she can build up a relationship with that person and develop a level of trust and relaxation. Some agencies operate a policy of changing the carer every fortnight. Often, elderly people find such frequent change-overs distressing, particularly if that person is undertaking a service that is highly personal, such as bathing.

In the absence of industry guidelines in this area the onus is on

Privacy and confidentiality   The client's right to privacy and confidentiality must be safeguarded. Information kept on clients should be made available to the client on request and should only be given to other agencies with the permission of the client. Member organisations should have appropriate written policies on confidentiality, which are binding on staff and should be made available to clients on request.

Comments and complaints The client's right to make complaints about the services she or he receives must be upheld. Member organisations must ensure that they have an effective procedure for recording and dealing with comments and complaints. Written details of this procedure must be given to each user of the service. Member organisations should assist clients to refer unresolved complaints to the UKHCA Complaints Procedure.

Non-discrimination Member organisations must not discriminate against clients on the grounds of race, nationality, religion or beliefs, age, sex or sexual orientation, or social standing; neither must they discriminate between clients who pay directly for the service and those who do not.

Assessment   Clients have the right to be involved in and comment on a careful and thorough assessment of their needs and wishes. Where an assessment has been carried out by a third party, the member organisation may have concerns whether it is appropriate. These concerns should be made known to the responsible party.

you, as the client, to make your wishes clear at the outset of any negotiations with an agency, and try to get some commitment from the agency to provide regular carers and to give a reasonable amount of notice when a change of personnel becomes necessary. Agencies will argue that it is difficult for them to provide guarantees because the stress of a carer's job makes it a notoriously high-turnover industry. However, one agency may be more receptive than another to giving some sort of undertaking so it is always worth talking to several.

Domestic staff agencies

As with nanny and domiciliary care agencies, it is advisable to choose a domestic staff agency that is a member of FRES as it will be bound by the FRES Code of Good Recruitment Practice, which stipulates that all members conduct their business ethically and to the highest standards. The code states that member agencies must ensure that their recruitment staff are adequately and appropriately trained and are fully aware of all relevant legislation relating to employment. FRES will also arbitrate in the event of any unresolved dispute between client and agency, and clients can make use of its complaints and disciplinary procedure when necessary.

The code stipulates that member agencies must take up references, endeavour to conduct face-to-face interviews with applicants, provide clear terms of business to clients at the start of business, ensure that applicants are suitable by taking detailed information from clients about their requirements and, if necessary, skill-testing the applicants.

What a domestic staff agency should do for you

You have a right to expect the following from the agency:

- written confirmation of terms of business before you use the agency, so that you can legitimately complain if the agency does not fulfil its obligations. Do not accept assurances over the telephone about what the agency will do for you
- to devote a considerable amount of time to covering all of the details of the position you wish to fill. Do not use an agency that will not take the time to get your job description right
- to check up on the details you have provided about yourself, perhaps by sending someone round to see you. This is particularly

important when you are seeking to fill a childcare position. The agency should be conscious of the safety of the female staff on its register. It should not send them for interviews with a family that it has failed to check properly

- to ask probing questions, such as 'Why did your last cook leave?' and 'May we contact him/her and may any job applicants contact him/her for advice about the job?'. The agency should try to discover whether you are an unreasonable (or worse) employer. If the agency has a responsible attitude towards applicants, it is likely to have a responsible attitude towards clients
- to check out applicants thoroughly. It should check the applicants' references, qualifications and work history before recommending that you interview them
- to observe a code of confidentiality for both you and the applicant. You want all the relevant information about both parties to be passed between yourselves, and you want both parties to be checked, but you do not want a recruitment consultant to be overly chatty on the telephone about an applicant's personal life, illuminating though this might be. If the consultant is indiscreet about the applicant, he or she will also be indiscreet about your business
- the agency's consultants to be courteous, helpful and sufficiently qualified and competent to give you advice on National Insurance, tax, legislation and other matters, particularly if you are a first-time employer
- to be sufficiently experienced in the employment of domestic staff to help you put together a job description and advise you about the current state of the labour market. For example, the agency should know that a British butler will cost, say, £30,000 a year plus perks or that the best cooks come from a particular college
- to respond to your request fairly quickly. Once you have decided to employ someone and have finalised the job description you do not want to wait two or three weeks while they search for applicants because they have no one suitable on their register
- not to advertise the position you are seeking to fill without consulting you first (this means all forms of advertising, including the Internet).

What a domestic staff agency will expect of you
Just as many people have had the misfortune of dealing with a bad

recruitment agency, so reputable agencies offering a good and reliable service have suffered from their encounters with unreasonable clients. Every contractual arrangement requires both parties to conduct themselves in a fair and reasonable manner, and you should be aware of what an agency's expectations will be of you, as the client.

An agency has the right to expect that:

- you will be courteous and helpful
- you will be honest in your description of the position to be filled, including the hours of work, type of duties and level of responsibility
- you will be honest about your family and financial situation
- you will settle your account with the agency promptly if it has provided satisfactory service
- you will inform the agency if you are dissatisfied and give it the chance to make amends before referring the matter to FRES or a solicitor
- you will take note of the agency's advice regarding the position you are seeking to fill. The agency may advise you that the hours you expect someone to work are excessive or the level of responsibility merits a greater salary. The agency's experience in such matters deserves your attention
- you will honour your agreement with the agency and not seek to employ one of its referred applicants privately, thus denying the agency its fee
- you will accept the agency's written terms and conditions by signing the appropriate contract or providing some other form of written acceptance
- you will be available to interview applicants as arranged and not fail to keep appointments
- you will not discriminate against applicants on the grounds of race, sex or creed
- you will treat all applicants with courtesy and respect.

What an agency will charge you

For nannies, au pairs and mother's helps agencies often charge a registration fee, which can vary from £15 to £30. On top of that are further fees for placements. For a temporary placement of three months to one year (most au pairs are placed for a year; a temporary nanny could be for as little as three months) the range quoted by agencies is enormous: from £55 (for a summer au pair placement) to £500 for a temporary placement of one year.

Permanent placements ('permanent' means the position is intended to be for more than 12 months) can vary from £450 to £1,000, plus VAT.

Domestic staff agencies charge roughly in the same range, depending on the type of position being filled. The placement fee for a cleaner, for example, may be as little as £30, whereas a fully qualified and experienced butler's placement fee could be £1,000 or more.

Chapter 5

The interview

Once you have a shortlist of applicants from an agency or have selected your own shortlist from the response to your enquiries or advertisement, you can conduct the interviews.

Security considerations

If you live alone, ask a friend or relative to be present at these interviews for reasons of security (see Chapter 4). Never let strangers know that you live alone, in case some unscrupulous individual tries to take advantage of your potential vulnerability. Be sure to let the interviewee know that people pop in and out throughout the day to check up on you. If the friend or relative you ask to attend the interview is currently acting in some capacity as your carer, he or she should in any case be involved in the selection process.

It is always advantageous to have someone else's opinion about a job applicant, suggest questions to ask that you have not thought of, and so on. In addition, should a misunderstanding or dispute of any kind arise from the interview, both parties will have a witness to what took place.

The applicant's security

As well as taking all necessary precautions to ensure your own safety, remember to give some thought to the safety of the applicant when you are arranging interviews: some people think that a hotel bedroom is an appropriate venue for a job interview, but it is not, and no respectable agency should allow its clients to hold, or attend, interviews in such a location.

If you live in a remote location – say, in the Highlands of Scotland – you may be forced to conduct initial interviews in the nearest big city before you narrow the choice down to a select few who will subsequently visit your home and children or elderly relative. If you are using an agency, it should be possible for it to provide a room in which you can conduct your interviews. If you have no alternative but to use a hotel, book a meeting room for the day and make it absolutely clear to applicants that they will be interviewed in a meeting room, not a hotel bedroom.

If interviewing young girls for a nanny or mother's help position you should be especially sensitive to their personal security. If you are a single father you could assure applicants and/or their agency that a woman will also be present at the interview (perhaps your mother, sister or previous nanny). Do not arrange interviews for too late in the evening, and encourage the applicant to bring someone along for support, such as her mother/father or a friend, who can sit in another room and have a cup of tea during the interview. This has the added benefit that you will meet a member of her family or see what sort of company she keeps.

When to involve the family

If you are the carer of an elderly or disabled person who is too frail to sit through lots of interviews, you may choose not to involve him or her at the stage of first interview. Similarly, if you are interviewing someone for childcare, you may decide not to involve the children until you have whittled the shortlist down to a choice of two, or have provisionally decided to accept one of the applicants but want to see her interact with the children before making a final decision.

When recruiting a cleaner, housekeeper or other domestic helper it is essential to interview in your own home. That, after all, is where they are going to perform their functions and they need to see the work environment. Again, be aware of security risks, and do not have extremely valuable items on display. Unlikely though it may be that a job applicant would pilfer an object while attending an interview, you do not want anyone to talk, however innocently, about your valuables to anyone else. Information picked up by a dishonest person in a pub or restaurant from a chatty cleaner could lead to your being targeted by burglars. Once you have decided to employ someone, you can then caution him or her about not discussing your home and its contents unnecessarily with others.

Defining the working relationship

The tone of the interview very much depends on the relationship you wish to have with your potential employee. If you want to have an informal arrangement you can introduce yourself by your first name and the job applicant will know that that is how he or she is to address you. If you want to keep things on a formal footing (as many older employers prefer) you should introduce yourself to candidates using your title (Miss/Mrs/Mr/Dr etc.) and call them by theirs. If the potential employee chooses to test the water by saying 'Oh, please call me Susan/Fred', you can reply politely, 'If you don't mind, I prefer to keep things on a formal footing and call you Mrs/Mr Brown.' If the candidate seems put out by this he or she may not be happy working for you.

What the employer needs to ask

The basis of the interview will be the job description you have worked out, either by yourself or in conjunction with an agency. It is helpful for the job description to be sent to shortlisted applicants beforehand so they can ring up to cancel the interview if the job is not for them, thus saving everyone's time. Those that are still interested should arrive for the interview with a thorough understanding of what you require in the way of services and be in a better position to ask intelligent questions.

The first thing you need to know is whether any of the tasks you have outlined in the job description could prove difficult for the applicant, or are simply tasks he/she would prefer not to carry out. It is irritating if this is the case, particularly if you have gone to the trouble of sending out the job description beforehand, but some people will expect to be able to negotiate over a few minor points if they are prepared to undertake the rest of the specified tasks. If you feel that the person is therefore unsuitable, you might be inclined to terminate the interview at this early stage, making it quite clear that it is all or nothing as far as you are concerned. However, if you are willing to negotiate on any of the contentious points, you could continue with the interview to determine whether the candidate has a willing attitude to everything else and is therefore still worth considering.

Requesting and checking references

You must ask for references and make it quite clear that you will check them. If someone cannot provide references it is generally wiser not to employ him or her. Some newly qualified applicants may be unable to supply an employer's reference, unless they have been on one or more work placements during their training period. In this case, ask for a reference from the school or college, as well as a character reference from someone who has known the applicant for some time.

In certain situations you might decide to employ domestic staff without formal references, such as a cleaner who is a friend of a friend and is looking to return to paid work now her children are at school. If there is some degree of personal recommendation, you might take a chance and employ him or her on a trial basis. It is still advisable to be cautious, however. Most people who are honest and reliable in their work should be able to provide at least one reference from someone who is happy to vouch for them.

When you check a potential employee's references, be persistent when you question the current or previous employer. Don't forget that some employers, in their haste to rid themselves of an unsatisfactory employee, will give staff good references in order to achieve an early departure. Asking detailed questions about the employee's attitude and attributes should help you to gauge the employer's degree of sincerity.

Knowing about someone's employment track record will also help you to assess whether that person is likely to stay with you for any length of time or whether he or she tends to flit from job to job.

Assessing an applicant's reliability

Reliability is the key factor with domestic staff, and the interview gives you the opportunity to probe a little and check this out. Before the questions begin, however, there are other clues. One is punctuality. If someone turns up late for the interview it is a bad sign. If the person does not appear to have read the job description or has lost it, that is another bad sign. You certainly cannot trust the care of your children or your elderly mother, say, to someone who is disorganised. Neither can you give someone responsibility for handling money or medicines if he or she is lackadaisical or forgetful.

Assessing an applicant's suitability for the job

Family and social life

Find out as much as possible about the backgrounds of the people you are interviewing. What are their hobbies? What kind of social life do they lead? What is their family situation? You do not want to employ someone to look after your elderly mother only to discover subsequently that she is also looking after her own elderly relative at home or has small children to cope with and frequently has crises in her own life to deal with, possibly at the expense of your relative's needs. Similarly, if you are employing a young person in your home, you need to know whether she spends her nights clubbing until 2 a.m. and is therefore likely to be turning up for work the worse for wear.

The degree to which this will affect your situation obviously depends on the job itself. You may, after all, be asking the young person only to walk your dog once a day and, as long as he can get himself out of bed by midday, his evening social activities need not concern you.

Health considerations

If you will be relying on an employee to provide continuous or full-time service, or will need him/her to do strenuous work such as lift an elderly person in and out of bed or the bath, provide round-the-clock childcare or do heavy work in the garden, then you need to know that the employee's health is good and has been up to the point of the interview.

Transport considerations

If the position is a live-out or part-time one remember to check how far away the applicant lives and what form of transport will be used to get to and from work. If you live in a rural area this is a major consideration. Someone who lives two villages away and is dependent on the two local buses a day to get from her house to yours may not be the best person for the job in terms of reliability and flexibility. In cities, you need to know whether the applicant is going to be travelling on public transport during the rush hour every day, causing you to worry and her to become frustrated and tired. Perhaps an adjustment in hours would solve the problem.

Religious, moral and lifestyle considerations

Find out whether the applicant has any strong religious, moral or lifestyle convictions that may make it difficult for him or her to work for you. For example, your elderly relative may have been advised by her doctor to have regular meals prepared of liver or other animal organs. The applicant may be a vegan with a horror of handling animal products. Similarly, you may be seeking to engage a nanny whose religious convictions might cause her to be uncomfortable about the fact that you and your partner are unmarried.

Assessing attitude and character

Unless you are a trained psychologist you are unlikely to be an expert in reading body language, but most people are able to read facial expressions and note reactions to certain questions or suggestions. A smile goes a long way to telling you that a person can make the effort to be pleasant. Whether or not a person is cheerful may not matter much to you if you are out all day and all they are going to do is let themselves into your flat and clean. But cheerfulness often goes hand in hand with an inclination to co-operate. People who have strong dislikes and grumble often are rarely the most helpful workers. If you are hiring a carer or nanny it is extremely important that the person is pleasant and sympathetic.

Initial impressions can be misleading because some people are very shy and appear to be lacking in warmth when, in fact, they are just nervous. If you conduct the interview in a pleasant and reassuring tone of voice, perhaps offering a cup of tea and making the interview seem more like a chat than a grilling, you may find that the interviewee gradually relaxes and assumes his or her normal demeanour. When interviewing a nanny who appears to be lacking in personality and charm, try introducing her to the children to see whether her character changes. Many girls who are drawn to childcare are often shy with adults but spontaneous and lively with children.

At the opposite end of the scale carers for elderly people can be overly cheerful and somewhat patronising to their clients, treating them rather like a nanny does her wards. It is essential to find someone who can be pleasant and chatty without adopting a patronising tone. Again, when interviewing someone on behalf of an elderly or disabled person, introduce the candidate to that person for a brief chat at some point and listen to the tone of voice she uses. If she treats the potential client as an intelligent person and the two of them can have a reasonable conversation, then you may have a possible match. If the carer is to provide meals for the elderly person, make sure that is discussed at the time and that the applicant has the necessary cooking skills.

With a straightforward domestic position you will be able to determine much about a person's character from the way he or she responds to your personal likes and dislikes over the way that things are done. An element of disagreement, however mild, on the part of the applicant during the interview – over your preferred cleaning methods, care of pets, frequency of cleaning certain items, ways of making beds and so on – is a good indication that once the person has settled into the job the disagreements will become stronger and you will end up exasperated with each other. That is why listing all of your preferences and demands and discussing them with an interviewee at this early stage is so important.

Always remember that you are the employer and are paying for a service that fulfils *your* needs. Unless you are being unduly unrealistic or unreasonable in your demands, you will find someone suitable in due course. Do not be intimidated when people tell you that good domestic help is impossible to find and impossible to keep, or panicked into employing someone who does not quite meet your criteria. Be patient, if you can. Investing some time in the selection procedure will pay dividends in the end.

What the applicant should ask

You want the applicant to understand your requirements as set out in the job description and to ask questions that clarify certain points. If an interviewee tells you, 'I'm not sure I really understand what the job entails', either you have failed to provide an adequate job description or the person is not as bright as you were hoping she would be. For example, included in your job description for a nanny is a requirement to 'take Naomi to playgroup'. You should therefore expect the applicant to ask where Naomi's playgroup is, how often she attends, what the hours are, whether the nanny will stay at the playgroup with Naomi or leave her there, whether you want the nanny to do other things during the playgroup times, such as housework or shopping, and so on. Questions such as these show that the applicant is intelligent and has thought about what the job might entail before coming for the interview.

Most of the questions you can expect from an applicant will be about the working hours, the fine detail of the duties and responsibilities, and the salary and benefits. Any job applicant who asks about the hours and the money *before* clarifying the duties and responsibilities has his or her priorities wrong. Anyone applying for the position of nanny or carer who asks about the money before enquiring about the children or people he or she is to look after should be shown the door immediately.

Negotiating terms

This is the part of the interview process that many people dislike most, particularly if they have had no experience of recruitment. It helps to have a pro forma contract to hand to which you can refer when you start negotiating. It is also useful to have gone over in your own mind beforehand the areas where you are prepared to be flexible so that you are not disconcerted by a suggestion from the applicant about hours of work or methods of payment.

For example, you may originally have wanted a gardener to work for two full days a week but the person you are interviewing, who seems to be just what you want, would prefer to do four mornings a week. This would mean that someone would be working in your garden almost every morning. Would this be an imposition to you or could you work around it? If you like to sunbathe on summer mornings or the children play in the garden every morning in the summer it may be inconvenient, whereas having the garden out of bounds for two full days a week might be less of a problem. Considering the possibilities beforehand will enable you to negotiate from a position of strength, and either accept the alternative suggestion or tell the applicant that, unfortunately, you cannot be flexible in this instance.

Employing full-time staff is like buying a house. You know what your maximum price is but you start negotiations lower down the scale. If the applicant is coming through an agency the salary may be non-negotiable. However, if you feel that the person you have interviewed does not quite have the experience you wanted but you would like to take him or her on anyway, try negotiating with the agency for a lower rate of pay on the grounds that the applicant has less experience than you wanted or some other drawback – and insist on a trial period.

The seller's market

Your negotiating position may be weakened, of course, by the fact that highly qualified and skilled nannies, butlers, cooks, chauffeurs or housekeepers are in great demand. You have to pay what the market dictates, and you will certainly have to offer more than the applicant's current or previous employer. However, you may find that you can increase the desirability of the job in terms of fringe benefits rather than salary. You may have fewer children than the nanny's previous employer, larger living accommodation for the housekeeper or a better car for the chauffeur to drive. You may be able to offer a private health plan or a non-contributory pension scheme. The position you are trying to fill may be more attractive to an applicant because it is local and means less travelling, you are prepared to accept flexible working hours, or the work itself is less demanding than his or her previous position.

Before beginning negotiations about money you need to ask one more important question: 'Why are you leaving/have you left your present/last position?' You also want to know the applicant's reasons for applying for your job. Is it for more money or for one of the reasons mentioned above: for example, that the job is closer to home, the accommodation is better, the hours are more reasonable, or the work seems less demanding. Once you know that, you have something to bargain with: for example, 'I'm afraid I can't offer any more than you are getting at the moment but, of course, there are only the two of us to look after. The workload would be much lighter than that of your present job.'

Discussing discipline

The reasons that would cause you to dismiss someone should be discussed frankly with the applicant during the interview. This could take the form of an example. You could explain that you dismissed your last nanny/nurse/cook/housekeeper because she was incompetent, her behaviour outside working hours affected her work, she was not punctual and so on. If you are engaging someone full-time and you are the employer, not a contractor, you should make it clear that you will follow the standard disciplinary procedure – i.e. a verbal warning, then a written warning, then dismissal. In most cases, the law requires that you give an employee two chances to redeem himself before you sack him.

Make it clear what sort of behaviour you would consider worthy of discipline leading to dismissal. For example, if you loathe smoking you have the right to state that an employee caught smoking anywhere in your house, even in the person's own room, would be given a verbal warning.

You have the right to dismiss someone instantly for more serious offences (see Chapter 10). Be very specific at the interview about what you would consider to be abuse of your children or your elderly relative. Surprising though it may seem, this is a grey area. A nanny should be told at the interview stage whether you allow your children to be smacked if they are naughty or whether you consider that to be child abuse. Indeed, she needs to know whether she can discipline them at all or whether she has to bring them to you every time they do something wrong.

Elderly people can be open to emotional abuse such as being shouted at, being humiliated if they have an accident, being ignored or being left alone for hours at a time.

All of these issues should be addressed in the interview so that the applicant understands your feelings on any matters relating to the care of your dependants.

Employees' rights and benefits

If you are interviewing applicants who have been sent by an agency the agency should have advised you about what rights and benefits you will have to provide. If the applicants you are interviewing have come by way of your own enquiries or advertisements you will need to be clear about what you are prepared to offer.

Among the rights and benefits you may need to discuss, depending on the job and your own circumstances, are:

- accommodation provision
- cooking and eating arrangements
- comings and goings from the house out of working hours (for a live-in employee)
- visits to the house by the (live-in) employee's friends
- access to any car that you may be providing for an employee's use
- private health cover or pension contributions
- holiday entitlement
- insurance cover
- maternity leave provision
- statutory sick pay
- notice period (for both parties).

Accommodation, use of car and house rules

Accommodation will be a key concern for a live-in employee, and Chapter 7 provides some indications of what different types of conditions employees are likely to expect nowadays. Refer to this well in advance of the interview and issuing of a contract.

Arrangements at meal times (whether the nanny eats with the family, or the carer takes her meals with the person in her charge, for example, or cooks for herself and eats in her room) need to be considered before the interview. If a car is to be made available for the use of an employee, or the employee has his/her own car, issues such as insurance (including insurance for the children/elderly person if the carer is to be transporting them) need to be sorted out.

If there are any other general house rules such as what time a live-in employee should be back in the house on working days and when friends are allowed to visit, again, try to take a view on these before the interview so that you at least have a basis for discussion, or know in advance that these issues are non-negotiable.

Private health cover and pension contributions

If you plan to offer the employee private health cover or pay pension contributions you need to ask whether she already has her own scheme(s) or whether your offer of these will be an extra benefit.

Holiday entitlement

The applicant needs to know how many weeks' paid holiday she will be allowed each year, and whether those holidays must be taken at the same time as your own holidays (if you are a working parent, for example). You also have to decide what happens on bank holidays – whether these are free days for the employee, and what arrangements you will make for cover, if necessary (agency carers, for example, tend to work bank holidays as normal but to receive double pay). Decide, also, whether you will want the carer to accompany the family, or her elderly client, on holiday and continue to work or provide companionship.

Insurance cover

You need to discuss both employer and employee insurance cover. An employer should be covered against claims for injuries caused by negligence in his or her home. For example, a gardener may be injured because the householder has provided him with a piece of faulty equipment and the gardener would be within his rights to sue. If you are employing one or more full-time or part-time staff you should take out public liability insurance. This is to protect the employer against claims from the staff arising from accident or injury at work. If the nanny falls down the stairs because your stair carpet has worked loose, for example, she is entitled to sue you for damages.

Employer's liability insurance is also needed, to protect the employer against the actions of his or her employees leading to a lawsuit. If your gardener accidentally chops down your neighbour's oak tree, or your chauffeur runs into someone else's car, you need to be covered against any action that might be taken by a third party.

All registered childminders should have public liability insurance, which covers them if a child in their care has an accident. It also covers loss or damage to the child's property or to other people's property damaged by a child in their care. The cover extends to another adult who may take over the care of your child in an emergency.

Nannies and nursery nurses are advised by their professional associations to take out a policy which covers them against claims of professional negligence. You could insist on this in your job description or ask the applicant if she would be willing to take out such a policy.

Maternity issues

If maternity leave could be an issue, this should also be raised at the interview. The right of all women to take 14 weeks' maternity leave and return to their job is not dependent on hours worked or length of service. Pregnant women have the right to time off for antenatal care and to Statutory Maternity Pay while they are on leave, which is paid by the employer but can be reclaimed from the Contributions Agency.

If the position you are interviewing for involves heavy work, such as lifting an elderly person in and out of bed, you need to discuss with the applicant whether pregnancy would render her incapable of doing that work. Make it clear to the applicant that you are not in a position to forbid anyone to get pregnant, but that it would be impractical for her to continue in the position if pregnancy occurred. This must be written into the contract of employment as a reason for dismissal, but it has to be made quite clear that dismissal would be on health and safety grounds only. It is advisable to take legal advice on this issue.

Statutory sick pay

An employee is entitled to Statutory Sick Pay (SSP) for up to 28 weeks of illness if it prevents him or her from working. Payment can be the statutory minimum (£55.70 a week in 1998) or the employer and employee can agree between them a weekly sum (as long as it is above the minimum). Again, this must be written into the contract of employment. SSP cannot be reclaimed by the employer. Employees not eligible for SSP are those who are over state pensionable age; those who have a contract for three months or less; those whose weekly earnings are below the lower earnings limit for NI contributions; those who were entitled to invalidity benefit, severe disablement allowance or maternity allowance in the previous eight weeks; and those who have done no work under their contract of employment – for example, an employee who falls ill on the day he or she was due to start work. An employer is entitled to end the employment if the illness proves to be long-term (for example, a stroke from which recovery has been poor) or the illness seriously affects that person's ability to do the job (for example, loss of sight by a chauffeur).

Termination of employment

You should also discuss how much notice both parties will give to terminate employment. This is not the same as dismissal but simply an understanding that either the job will come to an end at some point because the employer's circumstances change (say, the children no longer need a nanny, or the elderly person goes into a residential care home) or the employee wishes to seek employment elsewhere.

Probationary period

You should agree a probationary period with the person you intend to employ. This is in the interests of both employer and employee. With live-in staff, particularly, it is important to have a period to discover whether or not you can live together, as well as to find out whether the employee can do the job effectively or whether your job description accords with the employee's expectations.

Three months is a reasonable period and should give both parties enough time to make a mutually agreeable decision. However, the one-month notice period should still apply within the three-month period, to allow both parties to make satisfactory alternative arrangements should things not work out.

Interview checklist

At the start:
- terms of address between you and the applicant – formal or informal?
- punctuality of the applicant
- dress and manner of the applicant
- has the applicant read the job description?

Try to relax the applicant by being relaxed yourself.

Questions for the applicant:
- does the applicant have references?
- does the applicant have experience – if so, how many similar jobs and for what duration?
- where does the applicant live?
- why is the applicant leaving her/his present position?
- why is the applicant applying for this job?
- what is the applicant's family situation?
- what interests/hobbies does the applicant have?
- does the applicant have any health problems?
- does the applicant have any strict dietary, lifestyle or religious convictions that could have bearings on the position?

Negotiating salaries

Applicants should tell the employer what salary is being paid in their current or most recent position

Employer should ask the applicant why she/he wants the job – more money, better accommodation, more responsibility, change of scene, etc.

Employer should tell the applicant what is on offer by way of added benefits, such as use of car, paid holiday with the family, own telephone, pension scheme or private health scheme

Money and benefits should be discussed in relation to basic hours. Discuss remuneration for extra hours worked or services performed separately.

- does the applicant like (and is not allergic to) pets or could your [dogs/cats/birds etc.] be a problem?
- does the applicant like children/elderly people?
- has the applicant any questions about/problems with the job description?

Questions the applicant should ask you:
- what does the job entail (in detail)?
- how much responsibility will the applicant have?
- what are the likes/dislikes/mealtimes/activities/bedtimes/ medication etc. of the children or person the applicant will be caring for?
- what accommodation is provided (if the job involves living in)?
- what are the hours?
- what is the salary/benefits?
- what is the holiday entitlement?
- what other conditions of the job or house rules apply? (For example, will the nanny eat in her own room or with the family? When can her friends visit? Can the cleaner work flexible hours? Does the gardener make decisions about what to plant and where or defer to you?)

Contract of employment: points to discuss

Periods of notice to be given on both sides

Reasons for dismissal

Formal disciplinary procedures to be followed – i.e. verbal warning, written warning, dismissal

Confidentiality about your home and life to be part of the contract of employment

Probationary or trial period of employment to be worked

Statutory Sick Pay and, if relevant, maternity pay (potential employee must understand his or her obligations regarding notification of qualification for either of those rights).

Chapter 6

The employment contract

The law requires that an employee who works eight hours or more a week for an employer must have been given a written 'particulars of employment' document within the first two months of starting work. In practice, it is wise for both parties to agree the particulars of employment in advance and for each to sign a document to that effect before the period of employment starts. It is much more difficult to negotiate on contentious issues once an employee is actually working for you than to discuss and agree the requirements at the outset.

Even if an employee is to work for you for less than eight hours a week, it is advisable to have some form of written agreement.

A contract of employment need be no more than a letter which lays out all of the terms and conditions of employment, and is signed by the employer and read and countersigned by the employee. Each should keep a copy of the document for reference.

If you are using an agency, you should have a service contract setting out what level of service the agency is to provide, as agreed between you, in return for your paying a certain sum of money, settling your accounts on time and treating the agency's employees with consideration.

Childcare contracts

As noted in Chapter 2, in terms of the regulations governing their operations, registered childminders offer the best protection to children in their care. The National Childminding Association sells contracts which purchasers are free to copy and which are used by all of its members. Some local authorities also provide contracts which childminders in their area can use. The pro forma contracts provided by the National Childminding Association cover the following:

- the agreed retainer fee or deposit, should you wish to reserve a place for your child with a childminder who is currently fully booked but may have a place available soon
- the childminder's rates of pay (and whether she charges extra for unusual hours etc.)
- statutory holidays (including any religious festivals celebrated by you or the childminder)
- your own annual holidays
- the childminder's annual holiday
- occasional days off
- illness (arrangements for the child such as collection from school and care during the day, and whether this is to be done by the childminder or the parent)
- any extra hours that you may require the childminder to work and what notice of extra hours she would like from you
- playgroup or nursery attendance (what you wish your child to attend and when, and times at which the childminder is to deliver and pick up the child)
- any special requirements you stipulate for your child (discipline, diet, exercise, television viewing etc.)
- periods of review (at what intervals you and the childminder review pay and hours)
- terminating the contract (what periods of notice you both have to give and reasons for terminating the contract).

Other matters will need to be negotiated and put into the contract, such as whether the childminder will be paid by you during your holiday and her holiday. Most childminders suggest a half-fee arrangement at such times or, if they have school-age children themselves, agree to exclude the school summer holiday period from the agreement. Such arrangements vary according to individual circumstances.

If you are not using a childminder but are employing someone to look after children in your home, the contract between you, the employer, and your employee will differ in various respects. The organisation Parents At Work,★ which concerns itself with the needs and problems of working parents, produces a pro forma contract. It covers:

- salary
- probationary period
- hours of work (including any agreement about working extra hours, such as evening babysitting and occasional overnight care)
- holiday entitlement
- employee sickness (statutory sick pay, qualifying days, notification procedure etc.)
- maternity pay/leave
- insurance (employer's and employee's)
- termination of contract (how much notice is required on either side)
- confidentiality (on the part of the employee about the 'affairs and concerns of the household' in which they are employed)
- pensions
- grievances (the procedure)
- discipline (reasons which might give cause for instant dismissal or disciplinary action and the procedure for dismissal).

Contracts with nannies

A fully qualified professional nanny will expect a comprehensive contract. Any nanny who is a member of the Professional Association of Nursery Nurses will have been advised by the association to discuss the requirements of the job fully, especially at the interview, before deciding to accept it. She will have in her possession a model contract from PANN and she will expect to receive from you a contract which runs on similar lines. The model contract that follows is based on the PANN one.

Contract of employment: nanny

Date:

Name and address of employer:

Age(s) of child/children:

Name and address of employee:

Date of commencement of employment:

Job title:

Remuneration

The salary is .... per week/month* before/after* deduction of tax and National Insurance, payable on ....

The employer is responsible for accounting for the employer's and employee's National Insurance contributions and income tax.

The employer shall give the employee a payslip on the day of payment detailing gross payment, deductions and net payment.

The salary is to be reviewed once/twice* per year on ....

Length of probationary period:

Hours of work

(PANN notes that in a private household it may be difficult to define exact hours of work and free time, but that carers should not be expected to work unreasonable hours.)

Normal hours of work: from .... a.m. to .... p.m. daily, with .... free days per week and/or .... free weekends per month, from .... (time/day) to .... (time/day).

These arrangements may be varied only by mutual consent.

For occasional overnight care, by prior arrangement, extra payment, usually at babysitting rates, shall be paid, from the end of the normal working day up to midnight.

Maximum no. of hours to be worked per week:

Babysitting requirements (minimum of 24 hours' notice to be given unless an emergency arises):
(PANN notes that babysitting twice a week would be considered reasonable; anything extra, such as Sundays and occasional overnight duty, should attract additional reward.)

Holidays

.... weeks' paid holiday per year. In the first or final year of service the employee will be entitled to holidays on a pro rata basis.

(PANN notes that nannies should have at least four weeks' annual holidays plus bank holidays, discounting any holidays taken with the family. Statutory bank holidays that are worked should be paid at double time or the employee given double time off in lieu. Nannies should also be paid in their employer's absence: for example, if the employer goes on holiday but does not take her along, the nanny remains in the same employ and must therefore be paid. In cases of extended absence, the nanny should be paid a retainer. Paid compensation is not normally given for holidays not taken. Holidays may be carried into the following year only with the employer's express permission.)

Employee's entitlements

(a) accommodation (specify):

(b) bathroom (sole use/shared*: specify):

(c) meals (specify):

(d) use of car on duty/off duty*:

Petrol costs to be reimbursed at the AA-recommended rate if the employee uses her/his own car.

(e) other benefits:

Sickness

The employer shall administer the government SSP scheme in accordance with legislation. After 8 weeks of employment, the employer will pay the employee full pay for a period of .... weeks, then .... pay for .... weeks. After that period, only SSP will be due.

Termination

In the first 4 weeks of employment, one week's notice is required on either side.

After 4 weeks' continuous service, either the employee or the employer may terminate this contract by giving .... weeks' notice.

Confidentiality

It is a condition of employment that now and at all times in the future, save as may be lawfully required, the employee shall keep the affairs and concerns of the employer's household and business confidential.

Pensions

The employer does/does not* run a pension scheme.

Discipline

Disciplinary measures may be taken on any of the following grounds:

(a) causing disruption in the household
(b) incompetence
(c) unsatisfactory standard of dress/appearance
(d) conduct during or outside working hours that is prejudicial to the interests or reputation of the employer
(e) unreliable timekeeping or attendance
(f) failure to comply with instructions and procedures: for example, being unable to drive owing to a driving ban
(g) breach of confidentiality clause.

In the event of disciplinary action needing to be taken, the procedure shall be:

(1) oral warning
(2) written warning
(3) dismissal.

The employee should have the right to appeal to an agreed third party (see Grievances, below).

Reasons which could give rise to summary dismissal include:

(a) child abuse
(b) drunkenness
(c) illegal drug-taking
(d) theft.

Grievances

If the employee has any grievance against the employer, she/he has the right to seek advice (for example, from PANN, solicitor, nanny agency).

(PANN further notes that nannies are advised to have written details of insurance policies in place and written authority for duties such as taking children to participate in sporting activities, for example, swimming; they should also have written authority in the event of, for example, the absence of the parent(s) to act in their place.)

Signed by the employer: ....

Signed by the employee: ....

*delete as applicable

Contracts with au pairs

The system works rather differently for au pairs. As mentioned in Chapter 4, International Au Pair Association (IAPA) member agencies combine on one form assessment details and a job description, and ask the host family to sign that form, confirming that they understand all of the terms and conditions and undertake to be good employers. Similarly, the au pairs are required to sign an undertaking that they will behave in a responsible manner. Examples of both forms, which should ideally be signed at the time of registration, are shown below.

Au pair agreement

(1) I, ..., confirm that I have read all written materials provided by the au pair agency in my home country and my host country and that I fulfil all criteria. I understand that the au pair programme is a cultural exchange programme and not a contract of work. I am aware that being an au pair requires a high degree of both responsibility and flexibility and that I must take my duties seriously.

(2) I confirm that I have answered all questions honestly and that all information given in the application is true.

(3) After confirmation of placement, I shall stay in touch with my host family and shall inform them of my travel arrangements. I agree not to travel to my host family until I have received official confirmation of placement from the au pair agency.

(4) I shall familiarise myself with any visa requirements. I shall obtain necessary documents (e.g. a valid passport) prior to departure and shall not enter my host country without a proper visa (if required).

(5) I agree to cover all costs of language courses, travel to and from my host country (unless otherwise stated in the programme guidelines) and any debts incurred (e.g. telephone bills). I shall bring emergency funds with me, as recommended by the au pair agency, to pay for unforeseen expenses.

(6) I am familiar with and agree to abide by all programme guidelines and conditions, in particular those regarding the number and distribution of working hours, au pair duties, pocket money, free time, holidays,

language courses, transportation costs, insurance and the termination of the au pair arrangement.

(7) Upon arrival in my host country, I shall discuss in detail with my host family the daily or weekly routine and the expectations of both of us concerning the au pair programme.

(8) I shall carry out my childcare and light housekeeping duties with diligence. In addition to my au pair duties, I agree to keep my room clean and neat and to make a fair contribution to the cleanliness of the common areas of my host family's home.

(9) I agree to abide by all house rules set by the host family (e.g. use of telephone and facilities with the home, daytime and overnight visitors, curfew, smoking) during my stay and I shall behave in a manner which does not reflect badly upon my host family, au pair agencies or my home country.

(10) I shall seek the advice of the host family before administering any form of discipline on the children. Under no circumstances shall I hit the children or leave them alone.

(11) I shall discuss with my host family any arrangements for holidays well in advance.

(12) I shall make a concerted effort to experience the culture of my host country and to learn the language. I shall respect cultural differences and display tolerance towards others.

(13) I realise that the success of my au pair stay depends largely on me. I shall try to integrate myself into family life and, should problems arise, communicate openly with the family to seek a solution.

(14) If I have any problems or questions which cannot be discussed and resolved with the host family, I shall contact the au pair agency in my host country for assistance.

(15) I shall make every effort to resolve any differences with my host family. If no solution can be reached and I decide to leave the family, I agree to give advance notice (in accordance with the programme guidelines). During this period, I shall perform my normal duties and receive room, board and pocket money. If I ask to be placed with a new family, I realise this might involve my moving to a different city.

(16) I understand that I shall be expelled from the programme and must return home if:

- I fail to abide by this agreement or programme guidelines
- I falsify any information in my application (e.g. regarding smoking, childcare experience, health)
- I begin my au pair stay before receiving official confirmation of placement from the au pair agency, or the required visa
- I am responsible for repeated problems with several families
- I disobey the laws of my host country.

(17) I agree to leave my host country before my visa or residence permit (if applicable) expires.

(18) I shall not undertake any other paid employment and will perform only those tasks relating to the au pair programme.

(19) Should I decide to cancel my application, I shall inform the au pair agency at once.

(20) I shall notify the au pair agency immediately if there are any changes to the information included in my application.

Date: .... Signature: ....

Host family agreement

(1) We,[1] ...., confirm that we have read all written materials provided by the au pair agency and that we fulfil all the criteria. We understand that the au pair programme is a cultural exchange programme and not a contract of work and shall treat our au pair as a member of the family and not hired help.

(2) We confirm that we have answered all questions honestly and that all information in our application (including the description of au pair duties) is true.

(3) After agreement, we shall stay in touch with our au pair and shall arrange to pick her[2] up at the nearest airport or railway station on her arrival in the host country. We shall not encourage our au pair to travel to our family before we have confirmed the placement with the agency and our au pair has obtained a visa (if required).

(4) We agree to cover all costs for room and board for our au pair. We shall give her pocket money on a weekly basis (the amount to be in accordance with programme guidelines).

(5) We are familiar with and agree to abide by all programme guidelines and conditions, in particular those regarding the number and distribution of working hours, au pair duties, pocket money, free time, holidays, language courses, transportation costs, insurance and the termination of the au pair agreement.

(6) Upon her arrival in our home, we shall discuss with our au pair in detail our and her expectations of the au pair arrangement, including a written or verbal explanation of the weekly or daily routine, her precise duties, time off and advice on handling the children. We are aware that she will need time to adjust to her new surroundings and responsibilities and shall, accordingly, allow our au pair a familiarisation period.

(7) We shall give our au pair regular reports on her progress and performance throughout her stay.

(8) We shall set house rules (e.g. use of telephone and facilities within the home, daytime and overnight visitors, curfew, smoking) for our au pair.

(9) We shall discuss any arrangements for holidays well in advance.

(10) We shall make a concerted effort to introduce our au pair to the culture of our country and to assist her in the learning of the language. We shall also ensure that our au pair has the opportunity to visit a language school on a regular basis. We shall respect cultural differences and display tolerance towards our au pair.

(11) We realise that the success of the au pair arrangement depends largely on us. We shall try to integrate our au pair into our family life and, should any problems arise, communicate openly with her to seek a solution.

(12) If we have any problems or questions which cannot be discussed and resolved with our au pair, we shall contact the agency for assistance.

(13) We shall make every effort to resolve any differences with our au pair. If no solution can be reached and we decide to terminate the au pair arrangement, we agree to give advance notice in accordance with the programme guidelines. During this period, the au pair shall perform her normal duties and receive room, board and pocket money.

(14) We understand that our au pair shall be taken out of our home without a replacement if:

- we fail to abide by this agreement and programme guidelines
- we falsify any information in our application
- we are responsible for repeated problems with numerous au pairs.

(15) Should we decide to cancel our application, we shall inform the au pair agency at once.

(16) We shall also notify the au pair agency immediately if there are any changes to the information in our application.

Signature of host mother: ....

Signature of host father: ....

Date: ....

[1] For the purpose of clarity, the host family is referred to in this pledge in the plural form. All points also apply to single-parent host families.

[2] For the purpose of clarity, the au pair is referred to in this pledge in the feminine form. All points also apply to male au pairs.

Eldercare contracts

Contracts for care of the elderly or disabled could be with the local Social Services department (which will either provide the services itself, contract them out to a private care agency, or combine the two) or with a private agency or with an individual employee.

The contract with the Social Services department will cover, firstly, agreement to the care plan that has been drawn up, and, secondly, details of the department's agreement to supply you with those services. The contract will usually lay down a set number of hours of care a week, specify the rates, and so on. The care plan itself will be separate.

As explained earlier in this book, it is most unusual for Social Services departments to provide domiciliary services using their own personnel. Some departments, for example, operate their own home help service but contract-out all other services. What is of interest is the contract that exists between the department and its contractors, insofar as it relates to the quality of care provided to clients (or 'service users', in the parlance of some departments). All Social Services departments publish their own standards of quality of care and their contractors are obliged to meet those standards in order to be awarded the contracts to provide care in the community. Clients therefore have the reassurance that a quality control mechanism exists between the Social Services and the companies that they contract to provide services. Excerpts from the Standard Conditions of Contract for the Provision of Home Care Services issued by one county council and its home care providers are given below. It is your right to see any similar publication that exists in your local authority's area.

County Council Social Services Department: standard conditions of contract

1. Definitions

1.1 'The department' means the Social Services Department of the County Council.

1.2 'The service provider' means the person, firm or company with whom the department contracts for providing home care services.

1.3 'User' means a person provided with home care services, identified by the department.

1.4 'Home care' (also referred to as 'the services') means personal and/or practical support for users and/or their carers where such assistance is required. It includes, but is not limited to, such services as:

- personal care – assisting the person to wash body and hair; bath; brush teeth; dress; use toilet; get in or out of bed; eat and drink; night-sitting; respite care for carers; social and emotional care
- practical support – cleaning; washing; ironing; shopping; preparation of meals; collecting pensions; assisting with consequences of household emergencies, including liaison with local contractors.

1.4.2 Subject to separate accreditation by the department, service providers may be required to assist with the administration of medication.

1.4.3 'Personal care' shall not include care normally provided by qualified nursing or medical staff.

1.4.4 'Practical support' shall not include property maintenance services such as, but not limited to, gardening, house repairs, building and plumbing.

1.5 'Service charge' means the charge for services as specified in the contract, together with any additions or deletions agreed in writing under the contract.

1.6 'Contract' means the agreement between the department and the service provider for the provision of services, including all documents to which reference may properly be made in order to ascertain the rights and obligations of the party.

(Sections 2–7 inclusive are relevant only to the business dealings between the department and the service provider and are therefore not included here.)

---

8. Response times

8.1. The service provider shall make the services available when required to meet the department's operational needs and within a maximum of 24 hours from request.

9. Personnel

9.1. The services shall be managed on a day-to-day basis by a 'fit' person. 'Fitness' will be determined by reference to the following:

- relevant experience (business and caring)
- appropriate qualifications (management and caring)
- personal and professional references
- absence of relevant criminal convictions, including those generally regarded as 'spent' under the provisions of the Rehabilitation of Offenders Act 1974.

9.2. Service providers may employ staff directly or sub-contract the services to individual persons (home care workers).

9.3. Direct employees will have a contract of employment which includes a written statement of the activities and tasks they will be expected to undertake. Where staff are sub-contracted, such a statement must be provided by the service provider to the home care worker separately.

10. Identification of home care workers

10.1 The service provider must ensure that staff or agents employed to provide these services are readily identifiable and carry means of identification approved by the department.

11. Replacement of a home care worker

11.1 If the department requires a home care worker to be replaced, at least 24 hours' notice shall be given to the service provider and the home care worker but this shall not apply where the department finds the home care worker unsatisfactory. The service provider shall use every effort to find an appropriate replacement and in any case within 24 hours.

(Sections 12–17 inclusive, which are not relevant to the client, are omitted here.)

18. Confidentiality and access to information

18.1 The department and the service provider will ensure that satisfactory systems exist so that information classified by the department as 'confidential' shall be provided only to persons authorised by the department.

18.2 Both parties shall respect the user's right to privacy, and information classified as personal shall be provided only to any person or agency who in the opinion of the department has a valid reason for needing such information.

18.3 The service provider must comply with the Data Protection Act 1984 with regard to any computer records held.

18.4 The service provider must provide access to users to personal written information about themselves which is maintained by the service provider. Such access should be afforded on the basis of the Access to Personal Information Regulations 1989, which apply to local authorities.

19. Complaints and representation

19.1 The service provider will have a written complaints procedure made available to the user. Such procedure should take account of any disabilities or communication difficulties that the user may have. The service provider will keep a record of any complaints received and how they were resolved.

19.2 The service provider will make it clear that those users who remain dissatisfied may use the department's complaints procedure.

20. Equal opportunities

20.1 Within their chosen groups of users, service providers, when providing services, shall take into account the needs of the users and their ethnic origin, religion, disability, gender and sexual orientation.

20.2 Services delivered to black and minority ethnic users will take into account the user's culture, language, race and religion.

20.3 The service provider must provide services without discriminating between users, including those affected by HIV.

20.4 The service provider shall ensure that the staff working with the foregoing groups of users are sufficiently qualified, competent, experienced, instructed and supervised as the case may be to provide the services in a sensitive manner.

(Sections 21–30 inclusive relate to the business arrangement between the Social Services department and the contractor and are therefore not relevant to the client.)

Private agencies should operate a similar procedure to that of Social Services, drawing up a care plan in the first instance, then a contract incorporating the care plan. Many omit this first stage, however, and issue a contract which makes no reference whatever to the duties of carers. In such cases it makes sense for you, the client, to state these in writing: you can show them to the agency when you are considering becoming its client and use them again each time a carer is sent to you, so that your expectations are clear to all concerned from the outset and can be referred to in the event of a dispute.

Not all agencies interview their staff personally before recruiting them; others claim to have taken up references but have not in fact done so. Subject to the agency's rules on confidentiality, you have the right to ask to see the references of any care worker the agency is planning to send you. You can also ask to interview the person yourself before committing yourself to a particular carer. However, you may well be expected to pay any travel expenses incurred by the carer for attending the interview.

Carers from agencies may work two-week shifts, then move on to another client: some elderly people find this arrangement very unsettling, because it takes a while to get used to a new person, and then, just as they are getting to know the carer, it is time for her to move on. On the other hand, the fortnightly changeover means that if the two do not hit it off, they only have to endure each other's company for a comparatively short time. If the carer is absolutely unacceptable to the client, the arrangement can of course be immediately terminated, but the cost will have to be borne by the client. Also, it may not be possible for the agency to provide an alternative carer at the drop of a hat: much will depend on who is available. All in all, there is a considerable disincentive for clients to reject carers they dislike or whose behaviour is unacceptable – or, indeed, whose cooking is inedible.

Some agencies also stipulate that you must pay the travel expenses of the carer getting to and from your home at the beginning and end of the care shift. Be particularly vigilant about clauses in the contract relating to changeover (or travelling) days: you may find that you are expected to pay both the incoming and the outgoing carer for that day. Where the changeover is on a weekly basis, for example, this will represent a significant additional cost.

Some agencies also prohibit their carers from using their own cars in the course of their duties, obliging the client to use taxi cabs or arrange alternative transport to go shopping, for example, or indeed for the carer to shop on the client's behalf.

Before signing any contract with an agency, read its terms and conditions carefully so that you have a clear understanding of the commitment you are making.

The Continuing Care Conference's framework contract

The Continuing Care Conference (CCC)* is a coalition of commercial, charitable and public service organisations with a mutual interest in providing better care for current and future generations of elderly people. In April 1998 the CCC published a Framework Contract between Domiciliary Care Provider and Service User. The framework, or sample, contract sets out a range of possible terms and conditions that can be used in an agreement between client and provider (the private care company that supplies the home care workers). The CCC framework also provides guidance about what is good practice and what is an acceptable standard.

Part 1 of the framework contract is shown below. It forms part of a substantial information booklet which can be obtained free of charge from the CCC.

CCC framework contract between domiciliary care provider and service user (i.e. between agency and person requiring care)

Part 1

Legal context

This contract is between [name] (hereinafter called the user or client) and [name] (hereinafter called the provider) for the provision of services to [name] (hereinafter called the user).

This agreement shall be governed, interpreted and enforced according to the laws of [England and Wales/Scotland/Northern Ireland]. This contract sets out the terms under which you will be provided with services by the provider and under which you will be entitled to *care services*. You are advised to read it carefully before signing it and, if you feel it appropriate, you may also wish to obtain the advice of your next of kin, close relative, a legal adviser, an advocate or friend before signing it.

Prior to specification setting, [clients/users] must make available all relevant information, for instance as to lifestyle preferences, likes, dislikes, physical and other abilities and preferences as to the way in which care is given.

Specification of services

A specification of services has been prepared and is attached to this document which sets out the services to be provided. This will be agreed with the [client/user] and the provider before service commences to ensure that the user's needs will be met in relation to the care provided.

Trial period

The first [four] weeks of any arrangement shall be regarded as a trial period in order to ensure that the services are fully adequate and satisfactory to all parties concerned.

Any party involved may cancel the arrangement during this period by written notice of at least [48] hours.

Fees

The fees under this agreement will be at the rate of [£x] [per hour/day/week] payable [daily/weekly/monthly] by the [client/user].

The fees will be in respect of all those services set out in the specification of service.

The stated fee will include all elements of the charge to be made.

The provider will make an extra charge for any service or item not included in the specification if this is at the client's request.

The rate as defined in this agreement will be reviewed annually or more frequently if substantial changes in care needs and other services are demonstrated; or as a result of inflation; or specific statutory provisions coming into force. Rates may be increased or reduced according to the revised level of care required.

Where there is an increase or decrease in the rate, and where there is no change of the service level and provision, there will be a notice period of [six weeks] before any change takes effect.

Where the user does not agree to a fee change, he/she may terminate the agreement at the end of the notice period.

Facilities
The services provided will be as set out in the written specification of service agreed by the [client/user] and the provider.

The specification of services will include comprehensive details about the sort of help to be provided, its frequency, the time of its delivery and ways of bringing problems to the attention of the provider.

Staffing
The provider accepts responsibility for meeting the defined needs of the user and will provide suitably trained, sufficiently skilled, experienced and competent staff to meet the needs of the user whenever services are being provided.

Insurance
The provider will have the following minimum insurance requirements and be able to prove that it has them:

- employers' liability insurance
- public liability insurance (at least [£2 million] in respect of any one claim)
- malpractice/professional indemnity insurance (at least [£1 million] in any one year).

Any additional household insurance cover is the responsibility of the client.

Privacy and confidentiality

The provider will respect the privacy and confidentiality of the [client/user], who will be provided with a written policy on privacy and confidentiality which may be included as part of the specification of service.

The [client/user] will have access to any written information about him/her which is held by the provider.

Regular reviews

The specification of services will be drawn up in conjunction with the [client/user] and any carers, advocates and relatives as may be appropriate. This specification will be regularly reviewed by the provider in full consultation with the [client/user] and, where applicable, other appropriate external social or health care professionals.

A review shall take place initially [one month] after commencement of the service and at least [twice-yearly] thereafter. Additional reviews may take place when circumstances change.

Complaints procedure

The provider will operate a complaints procedure by which the user or someone acting on his/her behalf can make a complaint or suggestion in relation to his/her care or welfare throughout the length of the contract.

Termination procedure

The provider may terminate this agreement by giving notice of four weeks if:

- any amount due is not paid within 30 days of the due date
- after consultation, the provider is unable to provide the degree of care required by the [client/user]
- any other term of the agreement is breached by the [client/user] and is not capable of being remedied.

The [client/user] may terminate this agreement by giving notice of two weeks to the provider.

In the event of the client/user's death, this agreement will immediately terminate.

If you are employing a private individual to provide home care for you then you should incorporate your care needs into a straightforward employment contract (see below).

Contracts with domestic staff

If your employee is full-time, whether living in or out, the contract of employment should follow the basic guidelines set out in the model contract for nannies (see above), adding or deleting details that are relevant or irrelevant to the job in question. As stated at the beginning of this chapter, an employer is legally obliged to give an employee a contract if he or she works for that employer for eight hours or more a week. However, it is good practice to issue a written statement of employment to all employees, regardless of how few hours they work for you. The written agreement of both parties to terms, conditions, intentions and responsibilities provides protection all round.

The contract of employment should include:

(a) the name of the employer and worker
(b) the place of work and the employer's address
(c) the date when the employment begins
(d) the job title or description of the job
(e) the rate of pay and method of calculating pay (hourly, weekly, per job etc.), including details of overtime, extra work, different rates for different hours and so on. If the employee has come to you via an agency, you may find that you are charged double rates, for example, for hours worked on public holidays
(f) holiday entitlement and holiday pay, if any, including public holidays and religious festivals
(g) terms relating to incapacity due to sickness or injury, including any provision for sick pay
(h) details of any pension or pension schemes
(i) the length of notice required on either side to terminate the contract
(j) if the employment is temporary, the period for which it is expected to continue or, if a fixed term, the date on which it is to end.

Wages and overtime

It is important to agree all financial details before entering into an employment agreement. A housekeeper or cook might reasonably expect additional financial compensation if she has to cope with, say, six extra live-in guests during the school summer holidays. A chauffeur would merit a bonus if, say, you lent him to your visiting company chairman and he had to work a great many more hours over a certain period. A cleaner might expect to be paid double her usual wages if she had to clear up after a particularly wild party. Anyone tackling your laundry would probably charge extra for dealing with heavily soiled laundry during an elderly dependant's bout of incontinence. All such variations from the normal workload should be discussed and incorporated into the employment agreement, in order to prevent arguments at a later stage.

Method of payment

The method of payment should be agreed by both parties before the employment commences: do not assume that an employee will be happy to accept a cheque once a month (not everyone has a bank account). Your cleaning lady or gardener, for example, may rely on being paid cash-in-hand every week.

All employees are entitled to a pay slip showing any tax and National Insurance contributions that have been deducted, whether this is on a weekly or a monthly basis. If you agree with an employee that she will be paid in cash you must still provide her with a pay slip.

If you are housebound and/or elderly, however, and consider that it would be risky to have too much cash in the house, you will need to make it clear to a cleaner or other domestic employee that you are thinking of hiring that she will be paid by cheque.

With full-time staff, whether living in or out, you might want to ask whether they would like their salaries to be transferred straight from your bank to their building society or bank.

Holidays

If you are elderly or disabled and employing a care worker, someone will have to be found to care for you on public holidays or when your regular care worker takes a holiday. Fortunately, Social

Services departments and private agencies will provide all-year round cover for people in need – even on Christmas Day. If you are a dependent relative living with a carer who works, and the care worker cover is provided to enable your spouse/partner/daughter/son to go out to work, then you have to come to an arrangement whereby the care worker is never on holiday when the carer is away. One of the advantages of using agency services is that they will provide cover even when your regular care worker is on holiday. If you live alone and employ someone as a private employee, you can turn to an agency for temporary cover while your care worker is on holiday, or consider the option of a respite care facility.

In today's multi-racial society it is worth remembering that different ethnic groups have special religious festivals that they may wish to celebrate and cannot therefore be expected to work on those days. It is advisable to agree your own special needs as employer with your potential employee, too. For example, you may have advertised for a cleaner/housekeeper for three days a week and, if yours is an Orthodox Jewish family, one of those days will have to be a Saturday when you need someone to perform the domestic tasks that you cannot undertake on the Sabbath.

If your employee qualifies for holiday pay, this must be discussed and written into the contract of employment, too.

Incapacity due to sickness or injury

Where you are entering into a contract with an agency, it is a simple matter to make sure that the agency provides a replacement employee when your regular person is sick or injured. Where you have recruited your own staff, you need to decide, firstly, whose responsibility it is to provide a replacement in such circumstances (see Chapter 9). For example, your part-time cleaner may agree that, should she be ill or injured, her sister will come and clean for you instead. This would be her choice to keep the income coming into her family rather than lose it to a replacement that you may find during her period of incapacity. If your nanny is incapacitated, should it be her responsibility to ring her former agency and get a temporary replacement for you? Do you want her to interview the temporary replacement or would you prefer to take responsibility for this yourself?

You will need to decide your preferred course of action in these areas and discuss this with your employee before incorporating the substance of the agreement into the employment contract.

Full-time staff are entitled to statutory sick pay (SSP), but make sure that you have specified the payment details in the employment contract (you may, for example, have agreed to pay more than the SSP), as well as the rules and procedures for notification of sick absence. Details of maternity leave and pay should be specified in the same way.

Contracts with companies

In certain situations you might have a contract with a company to provide you with domestic services. For example:

(a) an employment agency that provides you with full-time, part-time, temporary or contract staff
(b) a laundry service
(c) a pool maintenance service
(d) a gardening service
(e) a house- or pet-sitting service
(f) a catering company
(g) a cleaning company.

All of these examples can be treated in exactly the same way: you tell the company what you want in the way of a service; it makes you an offer in writing of its service and its terms and conditions; you read the document and, if you agree with its contents, you sign a copy of the document and return it to the company. You have now entered into a contract and have accepted the terms and conditions of your service provider.

If you do not agree with the terms and conditions offered, write a separate letter to the company stating the points that you are rejecting and inviting it to make another offer. Do not sign the original contract and scribble amendments in the margin, because unless an authorised representative of the company is prepared to initial the changes this would not be taken as evidence of agreement by both parties in the event of a dispute.

Once you have agreed terms and conditions and both parties have signed, both parties should keep a copy of the contract for reference.

The contract should include reference to periods of notice required by both parties and should provide specific details in the section about the services to be provided so that failure to meet those criteria is sufficient reason for instant termination of the contract. For example, if a gardening company says that it will provide two people for two days a week to tend to your garden and, for several weeks, it fails to provide more than one person for one day a week, that would be grounds for terminating the contract owing to non-performance.

Other terms are implied in contracts, even though they are not written down. For example, under the Supply of Goods and Services Act 1982, the law takes the view that the following implied terms exist:

(a) where the contractor or supplier is acting in the course of a business, there is an implied term that he will carry out the work with reasonable care and skill
(b) any materials used by the contractor will be fit for their purpose and of proper quality
(c) where no time is fixed for performance of the contract, there is an implied term that the supplier will carry out the job 'in reasonable time'
(d) the contractor has a duty to take reasonable care of the goods entrusted to him and to protect them from damage, fire and theft.

However, it is best to ensure that all relevant details are included in a contract, rather than hope that the legal system will take care of any omissions.

Chapter 7

The employer/employee relationship

Having a good relationship with an employee requires more than just observing your statutory obligations as an employer and paying a good salary; an employer/employee relationship should be a working partnership based on good communication, mutual respect and trust.

People who have a high turnover of domestic staff that they have employed directly (rather than through an agency) usually have only themselves to blame. There are two main reasons why staff come and go with alarming frequency: first, because the employer did not make a good selection in the beginning; and second, because the employer does not recognise good staff when she (or he) has them, or know how to treat them.

Some families, worried by highly publicised tragedies in which nannies or au pairs have been accused of harming the children in their care, have taken to electronic monitoring of staff looking after children, without the employees' knowledge, to reassure themselves that their children are being properly looked after. Such tactics represent a total breakdown of trust between an employer and his or her employees, as well as being an extreme response to the perceived threat: of the estimated 200,000 nannies working in the UK in 1998, two have been suspected of being responsible for a child's death. Meanwhile, companies calling themselves electronic surveillance specialists have sprung up offering to install the required cameras, microphones and recording equipment.

Most organisations involved in childcare view electronic surveillance as an invasion of privacy, as well as an insult to the employee's character and professionalism. They fear that if the practice becomes widespread it will simply drive the best employees out of the marketplace.

Perhaps, like marriage, the domestic employee/employer relationship involving care for another person simply needs more work than most other other professional relationships, because of the close proximity in which the individuals concerned co-exist and the personal care being provided to the children or elderly people.

Setting up the right framework for the relationship can make all the difference. This chapter offers some pointers to getting it right.

Mode of address

In today's society, employers have domestic staff, *not* servants. Domestic service is provided either by people who are part of the local community, or by skilled professionals who are worthy of the same respect as any other employed person. This does not mean to say that you cannot have a formal, even slightly distant, relationship with your staff if that makes you feel more comfortable. If you prefer to be addressed as Mrs Brown or Mr Smith and wish to call your domestic employees by their titles in return, that should not prove a problem providing you made it clear during the interview that you would prefer a more formal relationship (see Chapter 5). Some people may object if, say, you insist on being called Mrs Smith but call your staff by their first names; such an arrangement may imply a degree of inequality in the working relationship that they find unacceptable; to others, it will not matter one jot.

Deciding on the form of address may seem a trivial point but it can lead to bigger issues. If you decide, for example, that everyone in the household will be on first-name terms, be aware that this opens the door to a greater degree of familiarity, which may prove uncomfortable later. Take care not to send out mixed messages, such as implying that it is acceptable for an employee to call you by your first name but showing disapproval when he or she shares a joke with you. Nor should you be hypocritical, telling your staff to call you 'Susan' in private but 'Mrs Smith' in front of guests. How you address each other will be governed to a large extent by the domestic service being performed: it is very difficult to be formal if someone is performing a personal function like giving you a bath, or the family nanny is taking her meals with you.

Some staff prefer to be addressed formally as it reassures them that you respect their position in their household. For example, a housekeeper may like to be called Mrs Smith because she feels that the title confers on her a degree of authority in the household. For the same reason, many butlers insist upon being called by their title ('Mr Hudson', or whatever) rather than by their first name. Whether or not your gardener or cleaning lady wants to be called by his or her title might also depend upon the person's age: older men and women are often keener on observing such formalities than are their younger counterparts.

CASE HISTORY: Geoffrey

Geoffrey has had the same cleaning lady for 30 years. She comes in three times a week to do his cleaning, laundry and ironing. They have always been 'Mr Stapleton' and 'Mrs Peters'. They have a formal relationship, in which long, personal conversations rarely feature, but a great deal of respect for each other. Geoffrey buys Mrs Peters flowers on her birthday and gives her a Christmas bonus. She makes him cakes every week, sometimes shops for him if he is unwell – she knows all his likes and dislikes – and, when he was in hospital, took him his clean laundry. Geoffrey attended her husband's funeral but does not normally involve himself with Mrs Peters' family.

Courtesy and consideration

More important than the form of address is the tone in which an employer and employee speak to each other. Conversation should be courteous and pleasant, from both sides. Staff who are spoken to in a dismissive and abrupt tone, without the common courtesies of 'please' and 'thank you', will respond by being sullen and resentful.

Assuming that you made clear at the interview your views on such matters as punctuality, dress, method of carrying out specific tasks, confidentiality and so on, and the employee responded positively, demonstrating agreement with your views and conditions, you may need to give only an occasional gentle reminder over matters of behaviour.

One very important point, which many employers forget, is to remember to praise as well as criticise an employee. It is unfair to notice only the mistakes your employee makes and never to give praise when he or she has done a job well or made a special effort. Everyone likes to be praised and an employee who feels appreciated will be more motivated to keep up a certain standard, as well as being happier in the job and more loyal to you as a caring employer.

Gifts and bonuses

If staff do work that is beyond the call of duty, consider giving small rewards. If your cleaning lady has to clear up after a particularly messy party, for example, you could give her a cash bonus and a bunch of flowers by way of a thank you. Giving your nanny a present from you and your young son after she has successfully potty-trained him is a pleasant way to keep goodwill flourishing. Giving employees a small present on their birthdays and at Christmas is another thoughtful gesture worth making.

Employers and live-in staff

The rules of behaviour for employer and live-in employee need to be strictly observed; otherwise, life can become unbearable for all concerned.

Privacy is essential for both employer and employee. A young woman who lives in your house as a nanny, au pair or mother's help has to feel secure and know that her privacy is respected. She should have a lock on her bedroom door, and, if possible, her own bathroom. No member of your family should go into her quarters uninvited for any reason – even small children should be taught to knock and wait for an invitation to enter. Neither should she have free access to the family's sleeping quarters, except for those of the children who are in her care.

She should be provided with a television in her own room so that she can watch programmes of her choice and not have to sit with the family in the evenings unless she chooses to do so. She should not, however, be banished to her room every night. You can extend an invitation to eat with you or spend the evening with you, but suggest, in a friendly way, that she might prefer to relax in her own room or go out in the evenings.

It is important when an employee is living in that all adults in the household are aware that they cannot wander around the house in a state of undress, leave the toilet door unlocked when using it or engage in any private activity that might cause embarrassment if happened upon. A live-in employee must be treated like a permanent guest and your behaviour modified accordingly.

Similarly, you should make your teenage au pair aware of the fact that she is not living with her own family and you would prefer it if she did not, therefore, come down to breakfast in her night-dress, cut her toenails in your kitchen or wander round the house with a face pack on.

Live-in housekeepers or couples who manage your house should, ideally, have a flat of their own, where they can retreat once their work is done and live normally, cooking their own meals and doing their own housework. You should also have rules about not bothering them after hours unless there is an emergency.

CASE HISTORY: Sharon and Paul

Sharon and Paul employed a Swedish au pair called Kyrsten who stayed with them for one year. A quiet girl who respected their household rules about behaviour and responsibilities, she had a limited social life – sometimes meeting other au pairs for coffee and a meal in London. As she had a boyfriend back in Sweden she chose to remain unattached while staying in England.

The only problem Sharon and Paul encountered with Kyrsten was her homesickness. She would occasionally become very depressed, even tearful, about being away from home. They suggested she return home but she was determined to stick it out. Sharon made some investigations and found out the details of a Swedish club that Kyrsten could join. Sharon then asked Kyrsten to help her make Swedish food for the family once or twice a week. Sharon and Paul also installed a VCR in Kyrsten's room, and, at their suggestion, Kyrsten's family sent over video tapes of

Swedish television shows and films each week. These measures were successful and Kyrsten was considerably happier for the remainder of her stay.

Social lives

Here again, consideration is the key. If you are living together in close proximity you need to think about the effect that your social activities will have on the others. Your nanny, au pair or mother's help is entitled to go out and see her friends, of course, but if she has to pass by your bedroom to get to her own you would be within your rights to request that she comes home at an hour which does not disturb you unduly. If she is going to stay out all night at a friend's house or at a party (which she is entitled to do if the next day is her day off), you need to know her plans and have a contact number, if possible, in case there should be some emergency. If she makes a sudden decision to stay out all night, she should telephone you and provide contact information.

If you intend to hold a party that it would be inappropriate for live-in staff to attend, you could offer them some money to pay for an evening out, or tickets to the cinema or theatre. If you are holding a dinner party for business contacts, you need to explain to your live-in nanny, as diplomatically as possible, that it would be preferable if she stayed up in her room for the evening, rather than going out, because you need her to keep an ear out for the children while you are entertaining. In this case, you should pay her baby-sitting rates, since she is being asked to remain on duty.

You will already have discussed during the interview your rules regarding your live-in employee bringing friends back to the house (see Chapter 5).

Above all, make it abundantly clear, particularly with young employees, what you consider to be reasonable behaviour and what you consider to be unreasonable behaviour. You may find this a great struggle if you have no experience of teenagers yourself and you realise that you are spending a great deal of time playing the heavy-handed guardian. If it becomes too much of a strain, you will have to talk seriously with your employee and possibly rethink your relationship or even abandon it altogether.

Communication

It is essential, in any relationship, that lines of communication are clear and kept open all the time. You must make time to speak to each other, even if you, the employer, are out all day and rarely see your domestic help, which may well be the case if she lets herself in with a key and does her job in your absence. A friendly telephone call now and then would suffice, to see how things are going and whether your employee has any questions, concerns or grievances. Constantly communicating in note form can give the impression that you are unapproachable, even stand-offish – a situation that can easily lead to misunderstandings and imagined slights.

Talking, ideally face to face, serves another purpose, too: direct communication makes it easier to make yourself understood – not just by foreign staff with limited English but by native-born UK staff as well. You may, for example, want a cleaner to clean something in a particular way which you need to demonstrate to her; or you may need to discuss with your nanny a sensitive issue such as disciplining the children – in which case, you want her to see that your expression is serious and you mean business.

Two-way traffic

Communication should come from both parties in the employer/employee relationship. You should be open to staff making suggestions about better procedures or practices, without their fearing that you might take umbrage. Encourage your employees to speak to you about problems or grievances as they arise, not to store them up until they become crises or festering resentments. Fostering easy communication will also enable you to make suggestions about the way that employees do their jobs without their perceiving it as criticism.

Here again, good communication skills will help you. It is always better to start your sentence with 'I wondered whether you had considered doing [the task in question] this way?' rather than 'I think it would be better if . . .', which is much more autocratic.

If this is the first time that you have employed someone to do domestic work for you – especially if you are a first-time mother and you are employing an experienced nanny – you may feel intimidated by your employee's greater experience and knowledge. Always remember that nannies, mothers' helps and carers for the elderly may be experienced and well trained but they are not the relative of the person they are looking after: you are. That gives you the understanding and authority to have the final say about the quality of care that is being given. If the carer, for example, should forget that and start usurping your authority, have a quiet word with him or her.

CASE HISTORY: Marianne

Having no female relative to help her, Marianne engaged a maternity nurse for six weeks just after she had given birth to her first child so that she could rest and recover.

Unfortunately, the nurse was very domineering, criticising almost everything Marianne did in relation to the baby. As a first-time mother, Marianne felt completely intimidated and lost a great deal of her confidence. She told her doctor that she thought she had post-natal depression; however, during the course of their conversation, the GP deduced that the attitude of the maternity nurse was the primary cause of Marianne's depression, and advised her to get rid of the nurse.

Marianne sacked the nurse and lodged a complaint with the agency that supplied her, explaining that the woman was very bossy and had caused her a great deal of anxiety. The agency removed the nurse from its books and Marianne gradually regained her confidence as a mother.

Changes in circumstances

It is only fair to keep employees fully informed of any major changes in your life that may be looming. If there is a possibility that the whole family will be moving overseas, or your husband is going to be made redundant and you will no longer be able to afford domestic help, or you are going to have another child, the nanny, au pair, cleaner, housekeeper etc. has a right to know at an early stage, so that she or he can plan accordingly.

You have a right to expect that your employees will do the same for you. If your nanny plans to get married or your housekeeper plans to retire, the sooner you know and can start looking elsewhere, the better. It is always preferable to interview for replacements before the present incumbent leaves so that he or she can explain to the interviewees what the job actually entails. You may also be able to arrange a change-over period during which the present nanny or housekeeper helps to train her successor.

Areas of sensitivity in employer/employee relations

Certain aspects of the employer/employee relationship can present grave problems to employers who are unaware of the sensitivities involved. The most significant of these are discussed below.

Sexual or racial harassment

A great number of complaints by employees about sexual or racial harassment arise from the employer's ignorance, lack of sensitivity or an arrogant assumption that everyone will share his or her sense of humour. It is extremely foolish, as well as offensive to the recipient, to make what you consider to be jokes or flippant remarks about sex, sexual relationships, someone's sexuality or someone's race and assume that they can see the 'humour' in your remarks. The Forth Bridge could be wrapped in industrial tribunal statements from employers claiming, 'I was only joking! I can't believe he/she didn't realise that!' You would be wise always to err on the side of safety when choosing topics for social conversation with an employee.

Religious affiliations

By the same token, you should never make jokes or flippant remarks about someone's religion; nor should you ever try to discourage a person from practising his or her religion while working for you, or express disapproval. This is something that should be worked out at the interview stage. If an Orthodox Jew says that he cannot do any work on Saturdays, or a Muslim girl is unwilling to cook pork sausages for the children, you have to decide whether that would disqualify them from the job you are seeking to fill or whether you can live with that arrangement. You cannot start complaining about observation of the Sabbath or dietary laws after making the appointment.

Political affiliations

Politics is just as sensitive an area as religion. You must decide at the outset whether someone's political affiliations are likely to affect your working relationship with him or her. For example, if you have friends who visit your house who are from ethnic minorities, there may be friction if your live-in carer is a member of the National Front and likes to make his or her views known. It may be less of a problem if your twice-weekly cleaner is a member of the same party, but should you take the chance? Even the normally good-natured exchanges of opinion between an elderly Labour-supporting employer and a Tory-supporting carer could become heated at election time. If you (or your elderly relative) have strong views on politics then it is a good idea to find out, at the interview stage, if potential employees have equally strong views.

Obviously, finding out this sort of information has to be handled delicately. You might approach the subject by stating your situation and asking if the potential employee would feel uncomfortable with that. For example, you might say: 'My husband is a Labour council-lor and we run Labour Party campaigns from this house. Would that bother you?'

Provocative behaviour

Practically every family that has ever had a teenage au pair under their roof has probably worried at some stage about the boys/men of the house flirting (or worse) with the au pair. So lay down rules to nip any potential problem in the bud. First, you should insist that the au pair dresses in a non-provocative manner – i.e. no tiny mini-skirts, no low-cut dresses, no cut-off tops, no wandering about the house in her underwear or night-clothes. Secondly, you warn your partner/hus-band/brother/teenage son to maintain a polite, friendly but not over-familiar attitude towards the au pair and, in particular, to refrain from suggestive banter or intimate joking. A teenage au pair, away from home in a foreign country, is very vulnerable. Teenage girls are prone to developing crushes on older men or, even worse, may misunder-stand comments and actions and become frightened. Any provocative behaviour, from either side, can escalate into a dangerous situation.

Misunderstandings are not confined to situations involving female teenagers: they can occur between employers (or members of their family) and employees of any age. Unguarded remarks can be construed as encouragement, over-familiarity as a desire to form a deeper relationship.

Alcohol and drug abuse

Signs of alcohol or drug abuse would be grounds for instant dismissal of an employee. The worst aspect of such problems is the length of time it will take you to find out. When you realise, to your horror, that for the last six months your children have been in the care of a nanny with a drug habit, you will feel ashamed and annoyed with yourself for not having been observant enough to notice sooner.

If you and your partner are working long hours and you rarely get the chance to see the nanny at close quarters, going about her job, the chances are that you may not notice any of the signs of drug-taking – a vacant expression, mood swings, poor co-ordination and so on. If you have any suspicions, however slight, of alcohol or drug abuse, you must confront the employee. You cannot afford to worry about upsetting your employee if your suspicions should prove groundless, particularly if he or she is employed in a caring function: the safety of your children or elderly dependant could be at risk. If the person denies using drugs or alcohol, ask if she would mind having a medical check as you are unhappy about her state of health. If the employee protests, contact the agency that supplied him or her (if any) and ask it to arbitrate. An employee who is innocent will stick up for her rights and you may end up having to pay some form of compensation, as well as making a formal apology; but it is better to make a mistake than to risk a tragedy.

CASE HISTORY: Caroline and Michael

Caroline and Michael employed a full-time live-in housekeeper who they noticed was becoming increasingly forgetful and vague. Eventually, they realised that she was taking more and more prescription painkillers for a persistent back problem, and she was unable to stop taking the drugs. They asked her to consult her GP and seek help but she continually avoided the issue. It became obvious that she could no longer function efficiently and had no intention of seeking help, so they dismissed her, giving her one month's wages in lieu of notice.

Money

Let us imagine that you have an employee who does a good job for you and whom you pay well but who cannot manage his own money – he gambles, he spends more than he can afford, he is constantly broke and is always asking you for an advance on his wages. You must have a serious talk with him, making it clear that you will not give him any more advances. Either he gets his debt problems sorted out or he leaves. There is no other way. Never allow yourself to be a 'soft touch' or to be bullied or wheedled into raising a salary to more than the job is worth.

Neither should you allow yourself to be bullied into giving a pay rise to your marvellous housekeeper who keeps hinting that she has been offered more money elsewhere. Make it quite plain that you pay what you can afford and no more. If she leaves you will find someone else. No one is indispensable, or irreplaceable.

Do not over-extend yourself by paying for domestic help that you cannot afford. Staff have a right to be paid on time for the work they have done, and should never be kept waiting for their money because you have mismanaged your own financial affairs.

Dishonesty

You do not have to put up with money, food, drink, household items or any other property disappearing. Neither do you have to put up with sudden increases in your telephone bills; nannies who sit your children in front of the television all day; chauffeurs who appropriate your car to use at other people's weddings; or gardeners who take your vegetables for their family table without permission. Any employee who steals from you should not only be dismissed but reported to the police. Any carer who is grossly neglectful or deficient in her duties should be dismissed and refused a reference, and a complaint should be lodged with the agency that sent the person to you. The gardener who helps himself should be reprimanded. Point out that had he asked you in the first place you might not have objected; it is the underhand behaviour that you will not tolerate.

Disapproval of an employee's friends/relatives

This is a difficult situation requiring delicate handling. Live-in staff have a right to have their friends visit them from time to time and you cannot prevent au pairs or nannies from having boyfriends. There is very little you can do if you dislike the boyfriend's personality, appearance or occupation except to exercise your right not to allow him in your house or around your children. Calmly state your position to the nanny/au pair. For example: 'I'm sorry. I respect your right to see whoever you wish but I'm afraid that I do not want your boyfriend in this house or anywhere near the children. Other than that you can see him whenever you are free, although I have to say that I wish you had a more suitable boyfriend.' You will be asked to explain why you do not like him and it is best to be frank. You cannot avoid the ill-feeling that will result, and your nanny/au pair may decide to seek another position. You may feel that this is a small price to pay for not having an undesirable person hanging around your home.

If your live-in staff have a separate entrance to their accommodation, in a basement or 'granny' flat, for example, you may never see their visitors unless they make their presence known in an intrusive way. Again, if problems arise, it is best to be frank: tell them you would prefer it if, when their friends visited, they did not play the music so loudly that you can hear it in your living room; or would they please ask their visitors not to sunbathe topless in your garden/smoke in the conservatory/wander into your part of the house, or whatever?

Outlining your standards and your requirements clearly enough at the interview stage to enable you to select like-minded staff, and making an effort to achieve good communication subsequently, will help to reduce the risk of your encountering the sort of problems discussed here.

Abuse of a dependant

Abuse of a child or elderly relative by a carer is possibly the worst situation with which you could be faced as an employer. Being sure is the first step – yet how much notice do you take of a child with an over-active imagination who says that the nanny smacked him?

How much credence should you give an elderly (possibly confused) relative who says that the carer does not speak to her all day/has not fed her/did not come to help her when she needed to go to the lavatory? When is abuse real or imagined? Some elderly people are very hard to please and complain continuously about carers, perhaps claiming that they lie, steal or are bone lazy. Children see things on television that they translate into their own lives and believe them to be real. Again, it is better to be safe than sorry: if you have any suspicions or worries at all you must discuss them with the carers.

The signs of child abuse, whether emotional, physical or sexual, will, according to the experts, manifest themselves through a change in the child's personality. A normally outgoing and chatty child may become withdrawn and fearful. The difficulty here is that a change in your child's personality may be the result of her distress at a change in her care situation, or because you have returned to work and she is left with a nanny for the first time. Such changes in personality, triggered by upheavals of this sort, will usually be temporary, however. Constantly reassure your child that she can always talk to you, that there is nothing that she cannot tell you, and that you will always protect her. Monitor the situation closely, talk to the nanny and the child, and make sure that you do not ignore any warning signs.

With carers for elderly people, you need to be certain that the carer is not intimidating the client in any way – and that the client is not terrorising the carer. At least with adults you can be reasonably sure that they will voice their complaints, following which you can investigate fully. One of the advantages of having a home care package through an agency is that you can ask the agency to assess the situation objectively and help you to make a decision about whether either of the parties involved is genuinely causing distress or whether the two are simply incompatible. Either way, the carer can be replaced with someone more suitable.

CASE HISTORY: David

David decided to employ a carer to look after his elderly mother during the day while he was at work. Disabled after a stroke and a little confused, she was taking a long time to recover and her speech was not very good. The carer, appointed via a private home-care agency, seemed to be well trained and highly efficient, but after about a week David found that his mother was getting very distressed every morning before she arrived. He could not understand what she was saying but he gathered that she did not like the carer. After a few days of this he resolved to make a surprise visit home during the day. He found his mother sitting in a chair in front of the television, which was blaring out a children's programme. She had wet herself and was sitting in wet clothing. A drink and a sandwich were placed on a table just out of his mother's reach and she had knocked over the drink in trying to get it. He found the carer upstairs on the telephone to a friend. The carer was dismissed on the spot. David called in Social Services and discovered that the agency he had used was not one of those that was recommended by the department. Social Services organised emergency care while the situation was sorted out. A proper care plan was drawn up and the department organised home care through its own sources to the satisfaction of all parties.

Parental jealousy

Jealousy is a very common problem between employer and employee where children are involved. Inevitably, if you are handing over your pre-school children to the care of a good, caring and responsible nanny, there will be occasions when you feel pangs of jealousy because your children seem to love the nanny more than they love you. It is not uncommon for a small child to run to the nanny when hurt or prefer the ministrations of the nanny when ill to those of the mother who is not the child's full-time carer. You will have to learn to live with this, but you do at least have the vital assurance that your nanny is doing her job so well that the children love and trust her.

However, be alert to the over-possessive nanny who actively urges her charges to ignore you in favour of her. A professional nanny should always encourage the children to love their parents and she should find little ways of reminding them throughout the day of the importance of their parents. Good nannies get the children to paint pictures for Mummy or perhaps telephone Mummy with their news. Good nannies make sure that the parents and children spend a little time together each day. Over-possessive nannies put pressure on parents to abandon their responsibilities as parents and volunteer to take over everything. Such nannies may try to persuade the children to have secrets from their parents and may also criticise the parents in front of the children.

What you are striving for is a balance between being confident that your children are well cared for and maintaining your own loving contact with your children. That may mean trying to take time off from work now and then to do special things with the children while the nanny has a day off. It certainly should mean trying to be home to have an evening meal with them or read them a bedtime story. The children should get the impression that their parents and their nanny are sharing the care as part of one big family.

Jealousy of a carer

Less common but equally painful is the jealousy felt by a son or daughter if his or her elderly parent seems to prefer the company of the carer to that of his or her own blood relatives. Relationships between elderly people and their children, sometimes strained already, are made all the more difficult by infirmity and illness. Some elderly people find it difficult to be looked after by their own children; it is hard for them to relinquish the role of being parent and protector and find themselves their child's ward instead. Elderly people often find it less inhibiting to be looked after by a stranger and may develop a close relationship with a professional carer which leaves their son or daughter feeling rather excluded.

All of the parties involved have to step back from the situation and look at it objectively. The elderly person should be made aware, if possible, that the son or daughter feels guilty and over-sensitive about a stranger being paid to look after his or her parent. The son or daughter should be reassured that the arrangement is working out well, and helped to understand that his or her parent feels less awkward being looked after by someone else. The carer should gently remind the client now and then of the importance of the client's own family, and point out that the carer is not a relative and seeks no reward other than the normal payment.

It is sometimes difficult to talk frankly to one's elderly parents about personal matters, and certainly it is hard to admit to one's elderly parent any feelings of jealousy, guilt or frustration over the care arrangement. Elderly parents may not even realise that they feel more comfortable being looked after by a stranger; they may simply find it more acceptable, without in any way implying any rejection of their children. The carer may not realise that he or she has become a cause of tension.

Sometimes an elderly person will be deliberately provocative and, say, try to play daughter off against carer, as a punishment for perceived neglect or out of frustration at the indignity of having to have a carer. A son, daughter or other relative in such circumstances should try to bear in mind that being elderly and house-bound can seem to be a demeaning position to find oneself in and emotions can run high. Making allowances is all that one can do.

The carer/client relationship

A live-in carer can become very close to his or her client, but the relationship should still be that of employee to employer. The carer must respect the client and the client's wishes, and the client should never be made to feel that the carer is performing an act of charity. Nor should the carer be made to feel like a servant or be openly resented or merely tolerated. The situation requires a great deal of mutual respect and understanding.

The client should honour the terms of the care contract and not expect a carer to do things outside his or her remit, such as clearing leaves out of the gutters, digging or walking the dog. If the contractual terms are respected no offence will be caused by the carer refusing to do other work.

Practical considerations

There are some practical measures you can take to make the employer/employee relationship easier, if you have the time, money and space in your home.

Accommodation for live-in staff Ideally, they should have their own quarters, away from your own, with their own entrance. If possible, an au pair/nanny should have her own bathroom and a bedroom near the children's rooms.

Transport for live-in staff A live-in nanny or au pair who is qualified to drive should (again, ideally) have use of her own car rather than borrow yours, so she will not be stuck indoors with the children or forced to use public transport when you need the car.

Food preparation for live-in staff Your child-carer may wish to prepare her own food, so you will need to agree times when she has use of the kitchen for, say, breakfast or supper in order not to get in the way of whoever is cooking for the family.

Bathroom for elderly dependant An elderly relative who lives in your house but has a daily carer or care staff coming in throughout the week should have his or her own bathroom, which may need to be fitted out with special equipment. Also, the carers may need to give baths at a time when other family members wish to use the main bathroom.

Gardener's equipment A gardener should have a full set of keys to garden sheds, greenhouses and, if necessary for access to water or cleaning equipment, the house.

Cleaner's equipment A cleaner should have a cupboard for cleaning equipment, to save rummaging through the kitchen, utility room and conservatory for different items. You should regularly inspect the cleaning cupboard and replace any items such as polish, bathroom cleanser etc. that are getting low, or ask the cleaner to let you know when supplies are running out.

Carer's equipment A carer should have a cupboard, or cupboards/drawers as appropriate, for such items as dressings, bath equipment, fresh bed linen and washing powder.

Cook's territory A cook should be left alone in the kitchen. No cook wants his or her employer hovering with criticism, comments or any other form of interference in the preparation of food.

Some of these things may seem trivial, but all too often it is the little things that grate on people and eventually wear away the goodwill between employer and employee.

Chapter 8

Employing foreign nationals

According to the Analytical Services Division of the Department of Social Security, the total number of known immigrants registering or re-registering for work in the UK during 1996–7 was 130,309. The Asylum and Immigration Act 1996, which came into effect on 27 January 1997, makes it a criminal offence for any employer knowingly to employ or offer work to a person who does not have the right to work in the UK. Employers face a fine of up to £5,000 for each illegal employee.

The Act applies to all employees, whether they are full-time, part-time, permanent or temporary. It does not apply to self-employed people who work for you as well as for other people (such as your shared nanny, perhaps). Nor does it apply to employees of contractors doing work for you (such as the one-man business that does your gardening) or to agency employees who do work for you (such as your home care attendant provided by Social Services).

Prior to 1996 the only way in which employers could check whether or not an immigrant had the right to work was if he or she produced a National Insurance number. This proved to be inadequate owing to the prevalence of forged documentation. For example, in 1994 Lambeth Council, in south London, was found to be employing more than 100 people using false identities or National Insurance numbers.

Now, the law requires that employers ask to examine a range of documents from a potential employee. These are laid out in the Immigration (Restrictions on Employment) Order 1996. They are:

- a document issued by a previous employer, the Inland Revenue, the Benefits Agency, the Contributions Agency or the

Employment Service which clearly shows the named person's National Insurance number

- a passport describing the individual as a British citizen or having the right of abode in or re-admission to the UK
- a passport containing a Certificate of Entitlement to right of abode in the UK
- a certificate of registration or naturalisation as a British citizen
- a birth certificate issued in the UK or Republic of Ireland
- a passport or national identity card issued by a member state of the European Economic Area (EEA) which describes the holder as a national of that state. EEA member states are Austria, Belgium, Denmark, Finland, France, Germany, Greece, Iceland, Ireland, Italy, Liechtenstein, Luxembourg, Netherlands, Norway, Portugal, Spain, Sweden and the UK
- a passport or other document endorsed to show that the person is exempt from immigration control or has indefinite leave to enter or remain in the UK, or has no time limit to his or her stay; or a Home Office★ letter confirming that the named person has such status
- a passport or other travel document endorsed to show that the person has current leave to enter or remain in the UK, and is not precluded from taking the employment in question; or a Home Office letter confirming this
- a UK residence permit issued to a national of a member state of the EEA
- a passport or other travel document endorsed to show that the person has a current right of residence in the UK as a family member of a named person who is a national of a member state of the EEA and who is resident in the UK
- a letter from the Home Office confirming that the person named is a British citizen or has permission to take employment
- a work permit or other approval to take employment issued by the Department of Employment
- a passport which describes the holder as a British Dependent Territories citizen and which indicates that that status derives from a connection with Gibraltar.

Employers are advised to ask for some of the above documentation when interviewing staff. If they are unsure about the validity of the documentation they can call a Home Office helpline.★

1

While the holder is employed as

....

at...

he/she is not subject to any condition or limitation on the period of permitted stay in the United Kingdom,

on behalf of the Secretary of State
Home Office

2

Leave to remain in the United Kingdom is hereby given

Until...

....

on behalf of the Secretary of State
Home Office

Date...

3

Leave to remain in the United Kingdom, on condition that the holder does not enter or change employment paid or unpaid without the consent of the Secretary of State for Employment and does not engage in any business or profession without the consent of the Secretary of State for the Home Department is hereby given

until...

....

on behalf of the Secretary of State
Home Office

Date...

4

Leave to enter the United Kingdom on condition that the holder maintains and accommodates himself and any dependants without recourse to public funds, does not enter employment paid or unpaid other than with

....

....

and does not engage in any business or profession without the consent of the Secretary of State for the Home Department Department is hereby given for/until

....

The holder is required to register at once with the police

5

Leave to enter the United Kingdom on condition that the holder maintains and accommodates himself and any dependants without recourse to public funds, does not enter employment paid or unpaid and does not engage in any business or profession, is hereby given for/until

....

The holder is required to register at once with the police

The first stamp (1) is an example of one that implies that there are no restrictions on the person's length of stay in the UK and he/she can work there indefinitely; (2) is an example of one that allows the person to take any work in the UK but not to remain indefinitely; (3) and (4) both show that the person can work only for a particular employer or do certain types of work; (5) is an example of a stamp that means that the person is prohibited from taking UK employment.

Documented National Insurance numbers

An applicant for a job must be able to produce an official document on which his or her National Insurance number is shown. For example, a document issued by:

- a previous employer
- the Inland Revenue
- the Benefits Agency
- the Contributions Agency
- the Employment Service (or its Northern Ireland equivalent).

Such documentation could take the form of:

- a letter addressed to the applicant
- a P45
- a pay slip
- a P60
- a NINO card (the new type of National Insurance card).

The Home Office advises all employers to take a copy of any document presented by an employee in order to prove that they employed that person in good faith.

Who may work in the UK?

The Act is not retrospective, so if a foreign national was employed before January 1997 he or she is unaffected. The Act does not apply to the employment of UK or Irish citizens, Commonwealth citizens with a right of abode in the UK, citizens of the European Economic Area member states, and members of families of all of the above.

Any immigrant with a valid work permit can work for the time specified on that work permit. Any domestic servant who has permission from immigration control to accompany his or her employer to the UK can work for that employer only.

Work permits

Workers who do not need work permits to take employment in the UK are:

- EEA citizens
- citizens of Gibraltar
- Commonwealth citizens who have a grandparent who was born in the UK
- Commonwealth citizens between the ages of 17 and 27 who come to the UK on holiday and take up employment for a limited time (i.e. 'working holidaymakers')
- persons with 'settled status' in the UK: people who have worked in the UK on a variety of work permits for a period of four or more years and have successfully applied for leave to remain indefinitely
- spouses and children under 18 of overseas workers who have lawful work permits.

The laws governing eligibility for a work permit do not cover the category that includes domestic staff, and it is unlikely that an unskilled domestic worker would qualify. The overriding criteria is that the work could not reasonably be done by a UK national, such as a highly technical, scientific or managerial job for which a foreign national has the qualifications and experience that his or her UK counterparts lack.

Bringing domestic staff back to the UK with you

If you have been living abroad you may be able to get entry clearance to bring domestic staff to the UK with you – particularly in the case of carers, if you can prove that the children or elderly relative are emotionally dependent on that carer.

Permission to stay will be granted for up to six months initially if your family is visiting the UK before taking up residence overseas again; or up to 12 months if you intend to reside in the UK permanently. The name of his or her employer at the time of entry will be noted on an employee's passport. If the employer intends to stay in the UK, employees can apply to the Immigration and Nationality Directorate* (part of the Home Office) to extend their stay. This is done by filling in form FLR(O) and, if the application is successful, permission to stay will be granted for a period of 12 months at a time.

If an employer decides to leave the UK permanently, any foreign nationals working as domestics for that employer will have to leave too, unless a member of the employer's immediate family, resident in the UK, can offer them a job. If the employer leaves the UK sporadically (on business trips, for example) but his main domicile is in the UK, the staff may remain for as long as their permission to stay exists.

On completion of four continuous years as a domestic, the employee can apply for leave to remain in the UK indefinitely provided his or her employer is still living in the UK and wishes to continue to employ that person.

Once an employee has received permission to remain for an indefinite period he or she is free to change employers. However, if an employee changes employer before four years have elapsed he or she will be committing an offence and permission to stay in the UK will be revoked. It is also an offence to take any other employment or stay in the UK after the permission to stay period expires.

Employees who lose their job with the family named may stay in the UK until the permission to stay expires on condition that they have sufficient funds to support themselves without taking any other employment or having recourse to public funds (e.g. housing and homelessness assistance, income support, job seeker's allowance, child benefit, disability allowance, housing benefit or council tax benefit).

CASE HISTORY: Tracy and Carlo

Tracy and Carlo have an au pair from Bosnia-Herzegovina – a friend of the family (no agency was involved) whom they decided to bring to the UK as an au pair to give her a chance to study English. They had a great deal of trouble getting her an entry visa from the British Consulate in Bosnia-Herzegovina. Tracy and Carlo had to provide several notarised letters stating that they would be financially responsible for their au pair and that she would live with them and be fed and clothed by them. After several months, once the consulate were satisfied that the girl would not be attempting to claim British state benefits or seek asylum, she was granted a visa for two years.

Abuse of overseas domestic staff

The current system, whereby domestic staff brought into Britain by their employers are prohibited from working for another employer, has caused considerable distress to some workers who have faced abuse and ill-treatment at the hands of these employers. Campaigners have been lobbying the government to change the rules to allow domestic staff who have been ill-treated to leave their employers and seek work elsewhere without jeopardising their work permit situation. While the government is believed to be reviewing the situation, no announcements of changes to the law have yet been made. Campaigners hope that changes to the law will allow overseas domestic workers to change employers providing that they stay in domestic employment and can produce evidence of ill-treatment.

Special rules for au pairs

An au pair placement is dealt with under slightly different rules from the above. An au pair placement is an arrangement whereby a single person aged from 17 to 27 comes to the UK to study English and lives for up to two years as a member of an English-speaking family. An au pair is allowed to help in the home for a maximum of five hours per day and must have at least two full days off a week. In return, an au pair is paid a reasonable allowances and given a room of her own.

Au pairs must come from one of the following countries: Andorra, Austria, Belgium, Bosnia-Herzegovina, Croatia, Cyprus, Czech Republic, Denmark, Faroe Islands, Finland, France, Germany, Greece, Greenland, Hungary, Iceland, Ireland, Italy, Liechtenstein, Luxembourg, Netherlands, Norway, Macedonia, Malta, Monaco, San Marino, Portugal, Slovak Republic, Slovenia, Spain, Sweden, Switzerland or Turkey.

Nationals of Bosnia-Herzegovina, Macedonia and Turkey must obtain a visa from their designated British Embassy or Consulate before travelling to the UK.

Au pairs, who must be unmarried with no dependants, may stay for a maximum of two years, after which they should *intend* to leave the UK. However, au pairs are entitled to apply to extend their stay if they were placed with a family for, say, one year, and wish to remain up to the two-year maximum by taking a placement for another year with another family. Although the initial permission to enter the country is given on the understanding that the au pair is going to be staying with a particular family, this does not preclude the au pair from changing families if things do not work out. The proviso is that the arrangements with the new family continue to meet the au pair placement requirements laid down under immigration rules.

Registration with the police

It is a legal requirement that all au pairs who have been granted permission to stay in the UK for longer than six months register with the police, which means taking his or her passport and two photographs to a local police station in the UK, filling in a form and paying a fee. This is not the same as a 'police check', which is covered later in this chapter.

Working holidaymakers

To qualify as a working holidaymaker a person must fulfil the following criteria:

- be aged 17–27 inclusive
- be a citizen of the Commonwealth, British Dependent Territories or British Overseas
- be seeking entry clearance for an extended holiday
- be unmarried or married to a person who qualifies for entry as a working holidaymaker at the same time, and both intend to take a holiday together
- have no dependent children who are aged five years or over or will reach five years of age during the holiday period
- intend only to take employment which is incidental to the holiday (see below)
- be able to support and accommodate himself or herself without recourse to public funds
- have the means to pay for his or her onward journey
- intend to leave the UK on completion of the holiday.

CASE HISTORY: Joanne

Joanne came to the UK in 1997 from Australia as a working holidaymaker. A fully trained nanny, she decided to join an agency as a temporary nanny to supplement her holiday money. She works as a 'holiday nanny' for the families of British expatriates who come home for short periods. She looks after a family's children for up to one month, until they go back to their posting or take up another one. She makes herself available for these short contracts on an occasional basis. For example, she will work for one month, have two months off during which she travels, then work for another month. All her jobs are live-in and she considers the pay to be good.

The maximum period a working holidaymaker is allowed in the UK is two years, and a working holidaymaker cannot work full-time for more than half of his or her stay. For the purposes of working holidaymakers full-time work is more than 25 hours per week. The law states that the work should be 'incidental' to the holiday – i.e. part-time or casual work, although provision is made for full-time work as long as it complies with the restrictions mentioned above. Additional restrictions on a working holidaymaker are:

- he/she must not engage in business
- he/she must not provide services as a professional sportsperson or entertainer
- he/she must not pursue a career.

Police checks

If you are employing a foreign national who has recently come into the country say, as a working holidaymaker, he (or she) should have a certificate from his country of origin that certifies that he does not have a criminal record. If he does not have one he can apply through his own Consulate or Embassy in the UK to get one.

Foreign nationals who have achieved 'settled status' – i.e. they have been working in the UK for more than four years and have been granted indefinite permission to stay in the UK – can apply at a local police station in the UK to have a check done that will show whether they have engaged in any criminal activities whilst resident in the UK.

Such has been the demand for police checks (or 'subject access' as the police term it) that the Conservative government considered setting up a Criminal Records Agency through which individuals and employers would be able to obtain information about criminal records in England and Wales. The present government has made no moves to implement this as yet, so application still needs to be made through local police stations.

At present, the procedure is as follows:

- applicant presents himself at a local police station and asks for a 'subject access' to be carried out under the Data Protection Act 1984
- applicant provides an ID document showing a signature (e.g. a passport, driving licence or medical card). The police will accept a legible photocopy
- applicant also provides a letter of reference and a photograph
- applicant pays a fee of £10
- the papers are passed to the National Identification Service in New Scotland Yard, which performs the search
- the Service will respond to the applicant in writing with details of criminal record or otherwise, usually within 14–40 days
- applicant then presents the information to the potential employer.

CASE HISTORY: Marita

Marita, from Sri Lanka, came to the UK as maid to a wealthy Asian family who took up permanent residence in London. Her permit to work was extended annually until she had worked there for four years, after which she applied for indefinite leave to stay. This was granted. Shortly afterwards, she left her employers because they disapproved of her decision to get married. She now works as a maid in a large hotel in London.

Rules for non-EEA students

Students who come from countries outside the EEA require permission from a local Employment Service Jobcentre (or the Work Permits Branch of the Training and Employment Agency) to take part-time or vacation work. Permission will be restricted to a specific job with a specific employer, and will be granted only if the Jobcentre is satisfied that the student is not taking work away from local applicants.

Any employer wishing to employ a non-EEA student must obtain form OSS1 from the Jobcentre. If you are intending to employ, say, a non-EEA student nanny for a short period as part of the work experience element of her course, you do not have to obtain permission for her to work; that is the responsibility of her college.

Asylum seekers

Anyone who is seeking asylum in the UK may apply for permission to work if his or her application has been outstanding for over six months. The person may then be allowed to work for any employer until the asylum procedure is completed, including any appeals.

Those who are appealing against a refusal of an application for further permission to stay will also be allowed to continue working in their present jobs until their appeal is heard.

Racial discrimination concerns

Since the Asylum and Immigration Act came into force in 1997, the Commission for Racial Equality has expressed concern that the Act will discriminate against non-whites, and has been at pains to point out that the Race Relations Act 1976 is still in force.

However, racial discrimination (but not victimisation) by an employer is not unlawful in relation to his existing employees or potential employees where the employment in question is for the purpose of a private household. In other words, in theory, an employer of domestic staff is entitled to state to an agency that he or she would prefer not to employ certain races, colours or creeds. In practice, a reputable agency would find this unacceptable unless there was a very good reason for it – for example, you are a Muslim family and you do not wish your child to be cared for by a Christian nanny.

If you are advertising yourself for, say, a nanny it would be permissible to state, for example, 'Muslim family with two pre-school children seek full-time nanny of same religion'. However, any publication would be within its rights to refuse to accept an advertisement that it deemed to be racially discriminatory, such as prohibiting non-whites from applying for your job.

The Commission for Racial Equality counsels consideration at the interview stage, and points out that employers should not make assumptions about a person's right to work in the UK on the basis of their colour, race, nationality, or ethnic or national origins.

You should make sure that an agency which is providing you with job applicants checks all the relevant documentation of overseas nationals and sends you a letter confirming that the documents have been thoroughly checked before the applicants come for an interview.

If you are advertising yourself you could state in the advertisement that 'overseas nationals are welcome to apply providing the relevant immigration documents can be produced on request'.

Discrimination can take another form: that of tailoring the salary according to the person's ethnic background. Some people consider that certain foreign countries are a source of cheap labour, and many agencies get requests for Filipino or Indonesian staff, for example, from employers who assume that these staff are going to be cheaper than their British counterparts. However, no reputable agency will discriminate between races; all the staff on their books will be valued according to their experience and skills only.

Employing staff abroad

Many people employ domestic staff when they are resident abroad, either as expatriate workers or as owners of holiday homes overseas. Most expatriates residing in foreign countries are able to afford the luxury of domestic staff as the local labour market has a plentiful supply of unskilled workers prepared to work for relatively low pay. It is best to ask your employer (if you are an expatriate worker) which agencies are the most reputable and to ask for guidance over local customs and taboos. For example, in the Middle East it is quite common for domestic staff to be flown in from countries such as the Philippines, Sri Lanka, Ethiopia and Indonesia. This is because strict Muslims do not allow the women in their families to work for foreigners. At the time of writing, agencies in Abu Dhabi, as an example, charged a fee for supplying a worker of between dhs2,500 and dhs4000 (6dhs = £1). This fee includes the air fare to bring the worker to the employer's home. The worker is paid dhs400–700 per month, depending upon nationality and experience, and the employer will also provide accommodation, medical expenses when necessary, food and clothing such as staff uniforms.

CASE HISTORY: Jeremy

Jeremy works for a British oil company in Oman, and he and his family have hired several staff through an agency recommended by the personnel department of his employers. They employ an Indonesian maid, a Filipino cook and an Indonesian nanny, all of whom speak good English and have been with the family for over a year. Jeremy and his family are considering applying to British Immigration to bring the nanny home with them when they return to England next year. Several other expatriates from the same company have done so and the arrangements have worked very well.

Finding a reputable agency overseas

Personal recommendation is by far the best way to find a good agency, but if you have to do the searching yourself the first thing to look for is an agency which is a member of a national employment agency organisation, which should have a code of practice or rules governing the operation of its members. Unfortunately, not all countries have such organisations.

The UK's employment agency organisation, FRES, is a member of an international organisation called CIETT* (the English translation of its full title is the International Confederation of Temporary Work Businesses). CIETT has a particular interest in workers who migrate to other countries to undertake temporary work. It also tries to encourage countries to set up national organisations to represent the employment agency business. At present, CIETT has member organisations from the following countries: Argentina, Australia, Austria, Belgium, Brazil, Canada, Curaçao, Denmark, France, Germany, Ireland, Japan, Netherlands, Norway, Portugal, South Africa, Spain, Sweden, Switzerland, United Kingdom and the USA. It has associate members in Iceland and Israel.

You can get a full list of members from CIETT, and can then contact those members in turn to get a full list of their member agencies.

Looking after the holiday home

Getting domestic help in a British expatriate community is one thing; buying an isolated farmhouse in, say, Tuscany or Provence is another. Depending upon how often you will be visiting your overseas home and what you plan to do with it when you are not there, you have several options:

- employ a full-time caretaker/housekeeper to live on-site all year round, if the property is big enough
- retain the services of a property management company, if such a thing exists locally
- ask the property agent who sold you the property to organise cleaning and maintenance
- ask a local lawyer to manage the property for you and organise cleaning and maintenance
- ask the nearest neighbours to recommend someone to clean and keep an eye on the place.

CASE HISTORY: Helen and Michael

Helen and Michael, both teachers, have a house in the Dordogne which they visit every school holiday. Initially, they employed a local caretaker/cleaner whom they inherited from the previous owners of the house, until she became ill and unable to continue working. As there were no property management companies locally Michael approached a local lawyer who had acted on behalf of the property's previous owners. He was able to find them a local couple to look after the house, keeping it clean, aired and in good repair. The lawyer attested in writing to the reliability and trustworthiness of the couple and agreed to take responsibility for the property in Helen and Michael's absence. They pay the lawyer a monthly fee and he pays the domestic staff.

Full-time caretaker/housekeeper

If you have a large property that you use frequently and do not intend to rent out in your absence, the best solution to prevent your property from being burgled or damaged when you are away is to employ a full-time caretaker or housekeeper. The advantages of live-in staff are that they are on hand immediately if anything goes wrong, such as the pipes bursting, and they will ensure that the house is clean and welcoming whenever you turn up. It is the most expensive option of those listed, but if you have invested a great deal of money in your ideal holiday home you may well deem it to be worth the extra outlay.

Property management company

Companies exist overseas that specialise in managing property that is to be rented out in the owner's absence. In fact, many modern developments in places like Spain and Greece are sold almost like timeshares, on the basis that the owners will be spending only six to eight weeks a year in their property and the company that built the complex will arrange the rental for the remaining weeks of the year or season.

If your holiday home is not part of a purpose-built holiday complex you could approach an independent property management company. Many people with experience in this area advise that it is best to approach one that is recommended by a lawyer, as the local lawyers will know whether a company is reliable or not.

It does need to be a local company, however. There is little point in hiring a management company in Barcelona when your property is in Malaga. If your property should suffer flood or storm damage, you want the managers to be on the spot as soon as possible, not three days later.

These management companies will usually hire local people to clean and repair your property, and perhaps even cook and do laundry each week for holidaymakers who rent your home.

Property agent

If you bought the house through an agent – e.g. an estate agent, lawyer or property developer – you could ask that agent to organise domestic help and caretaking. It is unlikely that the agent would manage the rental business for you, although he or she might act as your agent and point of contact should a problem occur.

Local lawyer

In many parts of Europe and the Mediterranean, local lawyers are the Mr Fixits of the community and can organise and manage just about anything for anyone – at a price. At the very least, they can usually recommend local people who are trustworthy and reliable to perform domestic tasks for you or to act as, say, a live-out caretaker.

Asking neighbours

Asking local people is usually the most productive route of all to finding domestic help. Neighbours may have domestic help of their own whom they are willing to share with you. Or their domestic help may have relatives who are looking for work. Enquiries among neighbours rarely fail to produce some valuable information.

Timeshares

Any timeshare agreement should include the provision of domestic help or, at least, regular cleaning and maintenance. You may have to pay a service charge for this. However the financial details are arranged, you should make sure that cleaning and maintenance are clearly written into the agreement, along with some kind of formal complaints procedure and guarantee of action if the services are inadequate. The property management company should also have sufficient insurance to cover itself and you against theft or negligence on the part domestic staff.

Employer/foreign domestic relationships

If you are employing a foreign national in the UK, you will probably need that person to have a reasonable command of the English language, particularly if he or she is in a caring role and may have to deal with emergencies. It may be less important for your cleaner or gardener to speak good English but you will still need to be able to communicate with each other and you will want to be confident that your instructions have been understood.

You may, of course, speak the employee's own language. Many au pairs are selected on the basis that the host family was once posted to or has relatives in a particular country and wants to keep up its command of that language.

Au pairs come to the UK primarily to learn English, and most have studied it at school and have at least a rudimentary knowledge.

It is not chauvinistic to expect staff to speak English reasonably well: British nationals going to work abroad for non-English-speaking families would be expected to speak the language of their employers.

Respecting customs and cultural differences

It is very easy, if you have no experience at all of a particular culture, to make awkward mistakes and perhaps to offend. If you are employing someone through an agency which has a history of supplying domestic staff from overseas, you could ask the agency's advice about the culture of the person you are about to employ.

When you employ people from a culture different from your own you should make time to talk to them, find out what is important to them and how your way of life differs from theirs. Anything that you can do to foster a working relationship based on mutual respect will be a positive step.

Chapter 9

Coping with holidays and absences

Once you have employed your domestic staff and they have settled into their day-to-day routine, sooner or later you will encounter an interruption: illness, or some family problem at home which leaves you suddenly without help, or holidays – theirs or yours. What do you do? Depending upon your individual circumstances and the contractual agreements you have entered into with your employees, several options are available, all of which will be explored in this chapter.

Be prepared for disruptions

It is always advisable when setting up your domestic help arrangement to set in place a back-up system in case the unforeseen happens. Put feelers out to friends: you may be able to strike up an arrangement between yourself and a friend that your nannies will take on each other's children if one of them falls ill – with the consent of the nannies, of course. You might be able to come to the same arrangement with a friend over cleaners or gardeners.

To cope in the event of a childcare emergency you may be able to arrange with your sister/mother/mother-in-law/other relative that she will come to stay while the nanny recovers or you find a replacement.

Whatever your domestic employment situation, it is wise – and in the case of home care and childcare, essential – to have back-up, someone with whom you have an ongoing agreement to provide help if the need arises.

CASE HISTORY: Polly and Adam

Polly and Adam engaged a full-time live-out nanny for their three children a year ago, fully aware that she had just got married and intended to have children as soon as possible. During their discussion at the interview, Polly and Adam told the nanny that she might bring any child she had to work with her and look after all the children together.

Six months ago the nanny told her employers she was pregnant. They have agreed between them that she will continue to work until her eighth month of pregnancy. Polly and Adam will hire a nanny on a temporary contract for four months, possibly a fully trained nanny who is in the UK as a working holidaymaker and is interested only in a short-term contract. The permanent nanny will come back when her child is three months old and bring it to work with her.

Coping with holidays

When you go on holiday, the ideal situation is that everything carries on as normal while you are away. If you have live-in staff, they will keep the place clean and tidy while you are gone, deal with the tradesmen and generally look after your home. With part-time domestics, a cleaner can come in and clean as usual, as well as feeding the goldfish or watering the plants, and your absence should make no difference to the gardener – indeed, you may need him/her to come in every day if it is the height of summer and you will not be there to water the garden. If you are taking a holiday but leaving behind your teenage son to revise for examinations, the domestic staff can take care of his meals, shopping and so on in your absence.

Taking staff on holiday with you

Staff that you may wish to take on holiday with you are carers, such as nannies, au pairs, mothers' helps, nurses and care attendants. You may feel that you want to take a holiday with your children and/or elderly mother but you cannot cope with all of their needs, especially if you want to have any sort of a break yourself. The solution, if the carer is agreeable, is to take him or her on holiday as well.

You could come to an arrangement whereby you give the carer a break now and then during the holiday, particularly if she is caring for an elderly person; the carer would appreciate seeing more than the inside of a hotel room or rented villa for the entire holiday. You could help out the nanny by holidaying somewhere where children are occupied by professional children's entertainers for some or all of the day. In return for free time during the day she could babysit in the evenings, allowing you and the other adults in the family to go out.

Holidays for everyone

Some parents with highly trustworthy nannies who have been with them for some time feel perfectly happy about going off on a holiday by themselves and leaving the children at home in the care of nanny. This would allow, for example, parents to take a skiing holiday by themselves during term-time.

Employers of full-time nannies usually try to write into the contract of employment that the nanny will take her holidays at the same time as her employers, so that replacement cover is not necessary. If you are sharing a nanny with another family or the nanny is part-time, however, such an arrangement might be difficult.

When the nanny takes her holiday at a time that does not coincide with the family holiday, parents will have to take time off work to cover for her themselves, employ a temporary nanny, or find alternative care for the children, depending upon their ages and the time of year. If the children are on holiday at the same time as the nanny, summer camps are an option for the over-8s. Staying with friends can be another useful fallback for children of school age. Staying with Grandma and Grandpa could be a further option for younger children.

Nannies who are foreign nationals tend to want to go home for a holiday every year and, if their home is in Australia or New Zealand, they might want to take all their holiday entitlement (the average is four weeks) at once. This is a long period over which to arrange cover if you are having to take time off work yourself or are relying on the children staying with family and friends. If you are planning to replace your nanny while she is away, however, you will find that four weeks is an attractive short-term contract for many temporary nannies.

CASE HISTORY: Pilar and Juan

Pilar and Juan, who come from South America and live in London, have three children aged between 4 and 12 and employ a full-time nanny, Angela. Juan is in the diplomatic service and frequently travels in Europe, taking Pilar with him. Sometimes he receives very little notice of his assignments. Pilar and Juan take occasional holidays, with or without the children. When they take the children, they usually take Angela too. When they go on holiday without the children, Angela looks after them in the London house, or in the rented house in the country if it is during school holidays. Angela manages to take about three weeks' annual holiday herself, though never more than a week at a time and always during term time. The housekeeper of the London house covers for Angela when she is away.

CASE HISTORY: Charles and Pamela

Charles and Pamela's large house in Kent is run for them by a couple who perform the functions of housekeeper and chauffeur/handyman. Charles was the chairman of a large multinational company before he retired. The couple, who have no children, take frequent holidays, most of which are to their villa in Corfu. Their housekeeper and her husband go ahead of them to get the villa ready and manage all the domestic arrangements for the duration of the holiday. They return to Kent one day before their employers to resume their usual duties. When the staff take their annual holidays Charles and Pamela usually go away at the same time and leave the house in Kent in the hands of a house-sitter.

Coping with a replacement carer

There is very little you can do about the disruption caused by your regular carer going on holiday and being replaced by a virtual stranger. A good agency will send the holiday replacement carer along for a few days in tandem with the regular carer so that you get a chance to know him or her and he or she gets a chance to understand the way your regular carer does things for you.

Comfort yourself with the fact that, rather than being in a residential home for the duration of the carer's holiday, you are in your own home, with familiar things around you, and disruption to your regular routine kept to a minimum.

Using a house-sitting service

Should your part-time cleaner take her holiday at the same time as you take yours, or you have no domestic help to come into your home to do a few chores and keep an eye on the place while you are away, you might consider using a house-sitting service.

House-sitting as a service has been available for quite some time, though until about 20 years ago it was known as 'temporary caretaking' and was used mainly by the very wealthy who spent a considerable part of the year in another country or another part of the UK. Today, house-sitting has become very popular, not least because it is looked upon favourably by insurance companies, some of which offer reduced premiums to people who use reputable house-sitting companies. Indeed, in the absence of an umbrella organisation for house-sitters, the best way to find a reputable company is to contact one of the major insurance companies. Guardian,* Norwich Union* and Eagle Star* are among the insurance companies that offer discounts to clients who use the services of house-sitters that the companies recommend.

The best house-sitting companies to use are those that are 'fidelity bonded'. This is a type of insurance cover commonly held by people who handle money, such as employees of banks and building societies. In essence, fidelity bonding reflects an insurance company's confidence that a house-sitting company thoroughly vets all of its house-sitters, taking up their references, conducting police checks and generally ensuring to the best of its ability that all are trustworthy people. One leading house-sitting company states in its literature that it 'investigates the backgrounds of sitters covering the last 20 years, takes up reliable references from past employers, solicitors, doctors, JPs etc. and makes detailed enquiries about county court and high court judgments, criminal convictions and bankruptcy'.

Other insurances that should be held by house-sitting companies are employer's liability, public liability and professional indemnity.

Another reason for employing a house-sitting firm that has been recommended by an insurance company is that, as in the au pair agency sector, a proliferation of small agencies has come into being, some of them run from home, which can disappear as quickly as they spring up. Some of these small agencies do not have full insurance cover, nor do they adequately check the backgrounds of the house-sitters they recruit; sometimes they do not even meet the house-sitter face-to-face.

CASE HISTORY: Edwin

Edwin, a successful businessman, is divorced and lives alone in Hampshire. When he decided to go on holiday recently he called a company of house-sitters, as he was concerned about his valuable furniture, gym equipment and electrical goods. He knew nothing about the company; he had picked up its business card at a local business advertisement point in a nearby supermarket. It did not occur to him to check whether the company was fully insured, could provide references and was reliable. He filled in a form about his requirements. The job was fairly easy, as there were no pets or houseplants to look after.

The first bad sign was that the sitter did not turn up before Edwin left for the airport. He had been told by the agency that the sitter would turn up an hour before he left and go through any details like switching on the burglar alarm, switching off the smoke alarm etc. Edwin telephoned the agency and said that he would leave the keys with a neighbour and ask the neighbour to brief the sitter. He phoned his neighbour from the airport and was told that the sitter had arrived and had been briefed.

However, Edwin arrived home two weeks later to find that the sitter was totally incompetent. He had kept forgetting how to switch off the burglar alarm and several times had set it off when he came back into the house and had to call the neighbour out to switch it off. Edwin also found some cigarette burns on his three-piece suite and discovered that the sitter had been using his very expensive gym equipment, in the course of which he had changed all the gearing on the bike and rowing machine. Edwin complained to the agency and demanded compensation. The agency apologised but did nothing more and, after spending several months pursuing the matter, Edwin discovered that the agency was no longer at its high-street address – it had disappeared without trace.

A good house-sitting company or agency operates along the following lines:

- you contact the agency with the full details of the job – size of house, dates you are going to be away, special responsibilities such as taking care of pets/livestock/pool etc.
- the company introduces you to the house-sitter who is most local to you
- you meet the house-sitter and discuss your requirements in detail (it is usual to pay the sitter's travel expenses for such a meeting)
- you approve the sitter and the company sends you a booking confirmation
- at this point, especially if you are a new customer, you may be asked to pay for the assignment in advance. This is to protect the company against time-wasters, but never pay for house-sitting in advance unless you are absolutely sure that the company is reputable, well established and not likely to disappear
- the company should ask you to draw up or fill in a checklist, which is given to the sitter prior to the engagement
- the sitter arrives at the appointed date and runs through the checklist with you
- you provide the sitter with a cash sum (between £3 and £8 per day) to cover his or her expenditure on food during the stay. Some companies offer the alternative of providing a fully stocked larder for the sitter instead
- you should give the sitter cash for any payments he or she needs to make on your behalf while you are away – e.g. paying the window-cleaner, gardener or milkman
- on your return the sitter should give you a full report on everything that has occurred in your absence and an itemised account of any expenditure.

What a house-sitter will cost

The basic charge for straightforward house-sitting is £20–£25 per day. Some companies have a minimum fee, to cover three or four days, that usually being the shortest period over which they will consider looking after a house. Most companies have a cancellation fee, which varies according to when you cancel. If you cancelled, say, one month before the planned house-sit, you would be charged a percentage of the originally agreed fee (amounting to perhaps one day's fee). The shorter the notice you give of cancellation, the larger the percentage you pay. Few companies will give you any refund should you return from your trip early, as the sitter will have already committed the time to take care of your property.

Looking after pets or livestock is usually charged as an extra, depending upon the size and number of animals. For example, looking after one cat might cost £1–£1.50 per day. A large dog might cost as much as £3–£5 a day as it would require a lot of exercise and attention. Rates for horses and other such animals have to be negotiated with each company. Many companies charge no fee at all for looking after small caged rodents or goldfish.

Briefing your house-sitter

House-sitters expect their stay to be reasonably comfortable. They do not expect you to turn off all the heating, for example, disconnect the television and video, or leave the fridge completely empty. They will expect to be able to make the occasional telephone call to their own home and family.

You need to leave the sitter all relevant telephone numbers in case of problems – plumber, gardener, vet and so on. Remember to tell the sitter if any of your animals has a particular medical condition, such as epilepsy, and leave instructions about any medication required; otherwise, you may be faced with a huge vet's bill on your return because the vet has been called in unnecessarily for an existing condition or because the sitter has not given the animal its usual medication.

Tell the sitter about any tradesmen that are likely to call during your absence – milkman every other day, vegetable delivery once a week, window-cleaner on Friday and so on. The sitter also needs to know of anyone else who has keys to your house and might turn up, such as a cleaner or gardener.

If you want the sitter to perform some special function, such as taking your car into a garage for repair so that the garage can work on it while you are away, this has to be agreed in the initial interview. Remember to put the sitter temporarily on your car insurance.

House-sitters usually regard taking care of houseplants as part of their general duties but if you have, say, a greenhouse full of rare orchids that need special care, tell the agency when you initially make contact because it will need to appoint a sitter with the necessary skills.

Gardening does not come within the normal duties of a house-sitter, but if you have to be away at a crucial time of the year when, say, your vegetables will need constant feeding and watering you may be able to negotiate a special rate with the company for that service.

Most house-sitters are aged between 40 and 65 and are active retired people. If your house- or pet-sitting task is a particularly demanding one, explain to the agency that you need someone very fit (perhaps to ride your horse every day while you are away) and they will match you up with someone accordingly.

What a house-sitter should do

The house-sitter's main obligations and rights are as follows:

- not to leave the client's home unoccupied for more than two or three hours during the day and never at night. The client should have the right to request complete 24-hour cover, in which case the sitter should not leave the house at all unless there is an emergency
- to be supported by a reputable company or agency that undertakes to provide an immediate replacement should the sitter fall ill unexpectedly during the client's absence
- never to make it known to callers, either at the door or on the telephone, that the client is away for any length of time
- not to have personal visitors at the client's home or to allow anyone inside it without an appointment of which the sitter has been notified by the client – e.g. an electrician coming to repair some wiring
- not to bring his/her pets or children with him/her; some companies request that couples be permitted to house-sit but in such cases charge the client for the services of only one person
- not to smoke in the client's home unless expressly permitted to do so
- to respect the client's wishes in relation to the care of pets. For example, if the client does not wish the dog to come into the house, the sitter should abide by the client's rules
- to be allowed to use the client's telephone but to make a note of all calls and pay for them

- to make a written record of any messages left on the answer-phone or given verbally at the door
- to make a written record of any loss or damage incurred to the client's property, and of who caused the loss or damage
- to make a written record of any expenditure incurred and, when asked by the client to make payments on his or her behalf, to ensure that receipts are received
- not to be asked to do, nor to undertake voluntarily, repairs to the property. If a problem should arise, such as a piece of equipment breaking down, the sitter should call his/her company and get permission to call in a repair man or, if it is not urgent, wait until the client returns
- to respect the client's home and property at all times
- to respect the client's privacy and confidentiality at all times.

Other assignments for house-sitters

Although the majority of clients use house-sitters when they go on holiday or away on business, there are other occasions when a care-taking service is valuable. For example, when someone dies and the family is awaiting probate, which can sometimes take a considerable amount of time, the empty property is vulnerable to vandals, squatters or burglars.

Similarly, if a family has moved into a new home but the old home is still unoccupied because of a break in the mortgage chain, a house-sitter can protect the property and be available, in consultation with an estate agent, to show prospective buyers around the property.

Using a pet-sitting service

A pet-sitter will come to your house at regular intervals while you are away and tend to your pets, but, unlike a house-sitter, does not stay in your house. Cat owners, in particular, seem to favour this arrangement, whereas dog owners, recognising that dogs are more sociable animals who need human company, prefer house-sitters.

Most veterinary surgeries display advertisements for pet-sitters, and your vet may be able to recommend a service based on his clients' experiences. Pet-sitters rarely carry the kind of insurance that house-sitters are obliged to have, but when you are giving someone the key to your house you need to be absolutely sure that they are trustworthy. You also want to know that they have a reputation for doing a good job and that they are skilled at handling the sort of pet that you have.

CASE HISTORY: Davina

Davina runs a pet-sitting business with a friend. They advertise through local vets, grooming parlours and dog-training clubs. When they set up, they took advice from their bank manager and took out insurance to cover themselves in case of any animal dying, being injured, stolen or running away while in their care. They show a copy of the policy to every prospective customer and also ask that their clients sign a contract which states that they will compensate Davina and her partner if their animal should cause injury to either of them. When they are contracted to look after an animal they visit it on several occasions before the actual pet-sitting takes place so that the animal becomes used to them. All of their contracts are live-out pet-sitting, except for rare occasions where an animal cannot be left alone all night. Once the contract starts they visit the animal several times a day: first thing in the morning and last thing at night, with other visits in between. Dogs are walked, fed, played with and settled down for the night. Cats are fed, let out, catflaps checked, litter trays changed and so on. Small animals are fed, cleaned and their bedding changed. Hens and ducks are fed and watered, locked up securely for the night and so on.

Davina and her partner are considering employing two other part-time people as work has become so plentiful.

Coping with the unexpected

Childcare cover

In the case of carers for children, bringing in a temporary replacement can pose problems, since children naturally become attached to one particular carer and sometimes react badly to their routine being disrupted.

CASE HISTORY: Petra

Petra has a full-time live-in nanny. When she engaged her nanny she agreed with her friend Helen, who also has a full-time live-in nanny, that they would ask their nannies to provide emergency cover for each other in the event of illness or an accident – a convenient arrangement since the two families live very close to each other and the nannies get on well together. Petra and Helen wrote the terms of the arrangement into their nannies' employment contracts. So far, Petra's nanny has taken on responsibility for all five children just once, when Helen's nanny had a stomach bug which lasted for four days. The nanny seemed to cope well, although it was term time and three of the children were at school for most of the day.

Sudden absences owing to illness or accidents are often the most difficult. The arrangements you make to cope in the nanny's absence will depend on its duration. A bout of influenza may last only a week and you may be able to ask a friend whether her nanny could cope with your children as well for that length of time. If, say, two of your three children are of school age, you could ask a nanny you are acquainted with who takes children to the same school whether she could manage your children for the week.

CASE HISTORY: David and Monica

David and Monica share a nanny with Ian, and the nanny looks after a total of four children in Ian's house. Unfortunately, no one had thought to put into place any back-up in case of the nanny's illness. When the nanny injured her neck in a car accident and was unable to work for four weeks, chaos reigned in both households: each of the parents had to take time off work at some point, Monica's mother had to move in for one of the weeks, Ian's sister came to stay for a few days (but had to bring her two children as well) and a local childminder found room for the children for the last week.

The experience was fraught for all concerned and made the children temperamental and difficult to control. Everyone was relieved when the regular nanny returned. The parents now plan to set up a reciprocal arrangement with another nanny to cover for each other in the event of a similar incident.

A broken leg which is going to be in plaster for, say, six weeks needs a different approach. You could contact the agency that supplied your nanny originally and ask it to find you some temporary cover immediately. You would not necessarily need a top-notch nanny as long as your existing nanny could supervise, even though she might be unable to do much else. Indeed, if she were able to supervise at all times you might even be able to ask a friend's reliable unemployed teenage daughter to be the nanny's arms and legs until she recovers from her injury. If your nanny is in hospital, however, you will have to use an agency to find a full-time temporary nanny.

Home-care cover

One advantage of home care provided through a care agency to the elderly or housebound is that there should be, written into your contract with the agency, an undertaking that the agency will provide a replacement for any staff who are ill or on holiday.

If you are caring for an elderly relative yourself and are suddenly in need of a break, are ill or have to go away on business, you can contact a charity organisation called Crossroads,★ which provides practical support to carers in England, Northern Ireland and Wales, and in Scotland through a separate branch (Crossroads Scotland). Crossroads operates more than 230 schemes supporting over 27,000 families a year through caring for carers. Among the range of services designed to give assistance to individual carers, the organisation can offer:

- domiciliary care
- palliative care (for terminally ill patients)
- 24-hour emergency respite care
- holiday respite care
- night care.

Crossroads also has specialist helpers to give respite care to patients with HIV, AIDS and Alzheimer's disease.

CASE HISTORY: Margaret

Margaret is a retired nursing sister in her 60s. Being healthy and active, she has registered with an agency to provide short-term respite care to the elderly and housebound, allowing their relatives to take a break. She usually works for two-week periods as a live-in carer, after which she takes time off to look after her own home and affairs.

The advantage of respite care at home is that it allows the relatives of elderly people to have a break without worrying that their mother/father/aunt etc. is being neglected, or has to go to a residential home and try to adapt to unfamiliar people and surroundings. Although some housebound elderly people, Margaret finds, actually look forward to their fortnight in a residential home, enjoying both the change of scene and the social interaction, some hate being away from their own home and settled routine. In such cases, temporary respite carers like her perform a very useful function, picking up from where the regular carer left off.

Domestic help cover

If your cleaner or housekeeper is ill or on holiday you have four options:

- cope with the work yourself
- let the housework wait until she returns
- ask if she has a friend or relative who could stand in for her
- employ someone else temporarily.

If your cook is ill, you can eat out or use the services of a catering company for any business or other dinner parties that your own cook would have handled. If your chauffeur is ill you can use the services of a chauffeured hire car company. If you need a temporary replacement for your gardener you can employ one of the many jobbing gardeners or small garden businesses, assuming they can fit you in.

Clarifying the terms of temporary employment

When you employ someone on a temporary basis – whether it is for an indefinite period to cover while your regular employee recovers from sickness or an accident, or a definite period such as holiday cover or your nanny's maternity leave – you must tell the temporary employee in writing that the job is for a limited period only, to avoid misunderstandings and discourage hopes on the part of the temporary worker that he or she will have a permanent job at the end of it.

Chapter 10

What to do if things go wrong

The best-laid plans, the most carefully thought-out job description, the most thoroughly vetted applicants and the (ostensibly) perfect employer/employee relationship will seem to count for nothing when things suddenly go wrong. While you cannot always be prepared emotionally for events taking a downward turn, you can at least know what to do and where to go for help and advice.

The Advisory, Conciliation and Arbitration Service (ACAS)★ recommends that, even if you have only one employee, it is advisable to set down, as part of the written terms and conditions of employment, the disciplinary and grievance procedures by which both employer and employee will abide.

ACAS further advises that, if an employee is dissatisfied or has a problem, he or she discusses the matter with the employer in the first instance, preferably with a witness present. If that fails to solve the problem the employee should write to the employer explaining the nature of the grievance, and should keep a written record of the work problem and how and when it occurs.

For employers, ACAS recommends that, except for instances of gross misconduct, employees who have failed in their duties be given a chance to redeem themselves by being given one verbal warning and two written warnings before the employer resorts to dismissal. Unless gross misconduct has taken place, an employer should never dismiss a worker without honouring the notice period required in the employee's contract or without pay in lieu.

Gross misconduct by an employee

An employee who commits an act of gross misconduct is entitled to no period of notice and an employer has the right to dismiss the person instantly. Gross misconduct includes abusive language; disloyalty to the employer; disobedience; drinking alcohol or using illegal substances while on duty; smoking on the premises (if prohibited in the employment contract); sleeping on duty; theft or other types of dishonesty; and violence. In terms of domestic staff who are carers either for either children or elderly people, you could add to the list gross negligence and physical, sexual or emotional abuse. Some of these acts will necessitate your involving the police; others can be dealt with in a variety of ways.

Abusive and/or offensive language

You do not have to put up with your employee using abusive or offensive language to you or anyone else in your home or using such language in public. If you discover this through, say, your elderly relative complaining that she finds her carer's language offensive or has been verbally abused for a bout of incontinence, or you hear your children repeating certain unacceptable words or phrases picked up from the au pair/nanny/mother's help, you should have a private interview with the person concerned and ask whether she has used such language in your absence. In the case of a nanny or other childcare worker you would be within your rights to dismiss her on the spot if you can prove this is the case, as anyone looking after children should know better. In the case of carers for adults it may be possible to give them another chance if they say they did not realise that their choice of language was causing offence, particularly as people's views of what constitutes abusive or offensive language will vary according to their age and experience.

CASE HISTORY: Adrienne

Adrienne, a divorced mother of two children, employed a mother's help to do some of the housework and care for the children after school. Her children began using swear words, which they had never done before, and she discovered that they were being allowed to watch unsuitable videos after school that were being brought to the house by the woman's boyfriend. She spoke to the woman about it and the woman became quite abusive. Adrienne banned the boyfriend from coming to her house but then discovered that the woman was taking the children to his house after school. She sacked the mother's help, paying her one month's wages in lieu of notice.

Actual verbal abuse, directed at children or the elderly, is an instant sacking offence. You should also complain to the agency that provided the carer since a person who directs his or her temper at those in their charge does not have sufficient self-control to do such a job effectively and should be prevented from making other people's lives a misery.

Disloyalty

In the context of employment disloyalty generally takes one of two forms. First, most employers would consider that a total disregard for confidentiality constitutes disloyalty. If you have made it perfectly clear to your employees that anything that takes place in your home is totally confidential and you have proof that one of them has gossiped about your household, you should confront the person in question with this proof and dismiss him or her instantly. There is no point giving the person a second chance in such cases.

The second type of disloyalty arises where, for example, your employee has approached your friends without your knowledge to try to get a better-paid job, or allows your friends to try to coax him or her away from you without telling you what has taken place. Such behaviour is very underhand and quite unacceptable.

CASE HISTORY: Maria and Janice

Maria and Janice live together in a permanent lesbian relationship. Both busy career women, they employed a part-time housekeeper to take care of their housework, laundry and ironing during the day. They discovered that the woman was discussing their private lives in the village after a friend of theirs overheard her laughing and joking with two other women in the local post office. Hurt by this display of disloyalty, Maria and Janice confronted the housekeeper, who was embarrassed but unrepentant. She was then dismissed.

Disobedience

In the context of employment two types of disobedience are the most common. In the first instance, the employee simply does not perform the duties he or she was asked to do. In the second, someone thinks that they know better than you and goes against your strict orders. This is not only irritating but can be very dangerous. For example, you tell your nanny, 'My son has an inner ear problem. Please do not let him play on the climbing frame because he could lose his balance and fall.' The nanny, however, decides there is nothing wrong with your son's inner ear and lets your son climb on the frame. Not only is she disregarding your wishes but she could be risking the child's safety because of her conviction that she knows best.

It would be, perhaps, rather harsh to sack someone for one act of disobedience, but when it occurs a second time it becomes apparent that this person is not prepared to make an effort to change and you should therefore part company.

Alcohol and drug abuse

Any employee found guilty of alcohol abuse or using illegal drugs while performing a care function in your home should be sacked on the spot. If you are leaving someone in charge of vulnerable members of your family, you clearly must be able to trust them to be fully in control of their faculties at all times. In addition, any employee of yours found to be in possession of illegal substances in your house is making you an unwitting accessory to a crime, which cannot be tolerated.

For employees other than carers, your response to alcohol or drug abuse may depend on the job they do and whether or not they live in your house. If your part-time cleaner has never missed a morning's work and has always done her job satisfactorily, you may take the view that her heavy drinking, in her own time, is none of your business. You cannot make such a judgement about someone who lives in your house, however. Your housekeeper may drink only in the privacy of her room or flat when she is off duty but, to take rather an extreme example, she could still burn down your house because she passed out with a lighted cigarette in her hand, or harm herself or your property in some other way.

If you know, or suspect, that your employee is involved in the purchase and perhaps even the sale of illegal substances, you must seriously consider calling in the police. This is never an easy decision to make and some employers would prefer simply to dismiss the employee, thereby getting rid of the problem, especially if they are worried that the employee might seek revenge on the family were the police to be informed. Much will depend on your relationship with your employee and your opinion of the extent of his or her involvement in illegal drugs. You may feel, for example, that an employee who is little more than a teenager is getting involved in drugs over her head, in which case perhaps a scare from the authorities would put a stop to it. You could have a confidential chat with the police, without divulging names, and ask their advice. If you explain your fears they may be able to investigate discreetly without directly involving you or your evidence.

It is possible for people to be addicted to prescription drugs and not realise that they have a problem until they start to become dysfunctional in some way. This situation has been known to arise among a small minority of care attendants who have taken prescription drugs to ease the pain of back, neck and shoulder strains caused by constantly lifting the elderly and disabled in and out of beds, baths and so on. The director of a large nursing home in the south of England says that a survey of staff conducted in 1996 revealed that several of them took high doses of painkillers and/or anti-inflammatories on a daily basis. Those staff that the employer suspected had become addicted were sent for therapy.

If you suspect that a hitherto loyal and reliable employee has developed a problem with either drink or drugs and, rather than dismiss the person, you want to help her to overcome it, the best approach is to have a heart-to-heart talk and try to persuade her to seek counselling or similar help. Your GP's surgery should have information on local groups that can help with addiction. It may be that the employee's dependence is the result of depression or some other illness. Either way, medical help is needed.

Smoking

Your attitude to domestic staff smoking in your home will depend on whether you are a smoker yourself and what function the person in question is performing. If you are a smoker, you may decide that domestic staff may smoke but impose certain restrictions: not in front of or near the children, for example, or not in the house at all. If you are not a smoker you may well decide against employing people who smoke, whether they say they will never smoke in your house or not. As one non-smoking employer put it, 'The trouble with smokers is that their clothes and hair smell of smoke, and even though my cleaning lady never smoked in my flat I could smell that she had been there.'

The point is, if smoking is forbidden in your house and in your employ, and you catch someone at it, do you dismiss the individual on the spot? Ten years ago the answer would have been no: you would have had to follow the correct disciplinary procedure of verbal warning, written warnings, then dismissal. Today, instant dismissal could be an option.

Sleeping on duty

No nurse or carer for an elderly person should ever sleep while on duty. One couple had a baby who, because he tended to stop breathing in his sleep, was wired up to a monitor. To help them cope with the strain of this, the couple engaged a night nurse through an agency. One night the nurse fell asleep so deeply that the parents heard the monitor alarm and arrived at the baby's bedside before she did. The baby survived but the couple sued the agency for supplying them with a nurse who was negligent.

The vast majority of life-threatening situations are dealt with in a hospital, of course, rather than in the home, but you may need to employ a nurse overnight if, for example, an elderly patient recuperating from an operation is incontinent and needs 24-hour attention. For a night-time supervisory and/or caring function, it is preferable to recruit through an agency rather than employ someone direct. The agency will then take responsibility for replacement in the event of a problem. If the person engaged is patently having trouble keeping awake and seems to lack the energy required for the job (possibly because he or she is 'moonlighting'), notify the agency that supplied the person and demand an immediate replacement.

Theft and other forms of dishonesty

If an employee is proved to be stealing from you, you will have little choice but to refer the matter to the police. Even if the person returns the goods, money or whatever else was stolen when you confront him or her, you should still notify the police because the person may well steal from other employers in the future.

Dishonesty in a domestic employment situation can take many forms, most of which constitute indirect theft: the chauffeur who hires himself and your car out for weddings when you are away; the housekeeper who buys food and household articles out of the budget you have given her, then returns them and claims the money for herself or sells the goods to her friends; the cook who hires herself out for private parties when you are away without your knowledge or permission; the nanny who pretends to pack up your children's outgrown clothes and toys for charity then sells them at a car-boot fair and pockets the money; the au pair who helps herself to the loose change from your purse (intending to return it, of course); the gardener who sells fruit and vegetables from your garden to his friends without your knowledge or permission; and so on.

While the amount of money or goods involved may be small, the fact that the employee behaved in such a devious manner is fatal to the employer-employee relationship, since it destroys the employer's trust in that individual.

CASE HISTORY: Alan

Alan, an unmarried sales executive in his mid-40s, employed a woman to do his cleaning and laundry. As he was often away, he gave her a key and she let herself in whenever she needed to. He began to notice that things were going missing: small amounts of money from his bedroom drawers, a watch, some cufflinks. He asked his housekeeper outright if she had been stealing from him. She was outraged and handed in her notice on the spot. However, she turned up the next day with her teenage daughter in tow and apologised, explaining that she had discovered that her daughter was the culprit. She offered to refund any money and buy new cufflinks and a watch if he would agree not to refer the matter to the police. Alan agreed and the matter was resolved.

Violence and fighting

No employer should tolerate violence, physical or verbal, in the home. If you discover, for example, that your elderly father's carer has a violent temper that he takes out on your father you must remove that person immediately. Make sure you have someone else with you when you confront the person, and if he or she refuses to go quietly say you intend to call the police – and indeed do so if it becomes necessary.

Emotional, physical or sexual abuse

If you employ someone in a caring role you must constantly be on the alert for signs of emotional, physical or sexual abuse. If your children or elderly dependant accuses a carer of some form of abuse you must confront that carer immediately. If your dependent relative is old and confused, do not accept the carer's explanations of accidents if bruises appear frequently. *Any* signs of distress on the part of children or elderly people should be investigated without delay. Never ignore them in the hope that your suspicions were misplaced.

Emotional abuse can be dealt with by removing the carer and making a strong complaint to the agency concerned. Physical or sexual abuse are matters for the police. If it transpires that your child was not actually abused but you firmly believe it would have been just a matter of time as the intent was there and the signs were strong, you may wish to take matters no further as far as your own child is concerned, but you must bring the full force of your distress and anger to bear on any agency responsible for providing or employing the person in question. You would be within your rights to ask the agency for a written undertaking that it will not employ this person anywhere near children again. Once you have that written confirmation, you can pass it to the police and ask them to keep the name on file in case anything similar should happen involving that person. If, when you contact the police, you discover that the person in question has one or more previous convictions for child abuse but the agency had failed to check whether the person had a criminal record, you can sue the agency for negligence.

If the abuse is of an adult by his or her carer, call the police and let them investigate fully. If the abused person is elderly and frail, make it clear to the police that that is the situation. A medical investigation may be necessary to check for evidence of sexual assault or signs of physical abuse such as bruises or burns,. The agency that provided the carer should be involved, as well as Social Services (they could be one and the same). At the same time, ask Social Services to provide counselling to enable you and your dependant to survive the abuse ordeal and its aftermath.

Long-term sickness

It is possible that your domestic employee could fall prey to a long-term illness. As no specific laws on dismissal for illness exist in the UK, most authoritative bodies that give advice to employers suggest that good practice be based upon the decisions of industrial tribunals made over many years. Initially, try to keep in constant touch with the employee to find out how his or her condition is progressing. Then, consult the employee's doctor, with the (preferably written) permission of the employee, to find out what the prospects are of the employee returning to work in the future.

If, after consultation with the employee and his or her doctor, you are forced to conclude reluctantly that the existing employment can no longer continue and you have no suitable alternative employment to offer the employee, you will have to explain this to the employee in writing and ensure that the agreed period of notice in his or her employment contract is covered by the wages in lieu that you are enclosing.

The decision to let someone go has to be based on what duties need to be performed. For example, a carer for an adult who has been away from work for several weeks because of a bad back will clearly be unable to continue in a job that requires a lot of heavy lifting. If you can offer no suitable alternative employment you will have to replace that person.

Persistent short-term illness

If your employee is frequently away from work for short periods because of illness, the person is either a malingerer or a hypochondriac, or genuinely suffers from a recurring illness of some kind, such as severe migraines. If the employee insists that he or she has a recurring illness you should follow the procedure outlined above for long-term illness; otherwise, in the event that the employee brings an action against you, an industrial tribunal might decide that you have dismissed someone unfairly.

CASE HISTORY: Daphne

Daphne, housebound and in her 80s, employs a full-time carer. The carer, a former geriatric nurse, is Daphne's own employee, not contracted through an agency. When she began to have problems with an old neck and shoulder injury and to take the odd day off, which escalated into her being unable to work on at least two full days each week, Daphne found it increasingly difficult to cope. As her son-in-law was a personnel manager, she enlisted his help in ascertaining whether the carer's medical problem was a long-term one. He discovered that the woman's doctor had referred her for cortisone injections and investigations with a view to surgery. It was obvious that her long-term prospects for work were not good, so he wrote the carer a formal letter of dismissal on Daphne's behalf. The woman objected but, after a visit from an arbitrator who advised that her case was not strong, she decided to drop the matter.

Inability to do the job

'Inability to do the job' may sound like a useful catch-all description that will allow you to get rid of any employee you wish to, but an industrial tribunal will expect your reasons to be very specific. For example, if a chauffeur were to lose his driving licence he would clearly be unable to do his job and you would have a clear-cut reason for dismissing him.

The 'inability to do the job' criterion would also apply to an employee, such as a nanny, who you felt was not well enough qualified to do the job for which you had hired her. This may be because she misrepresented herself when she applied for the job, or it may be that you have a child with special needs, for example, who requires more expert supervision than your nanny can give him.

Always write a probationary period into your employment contracts: in almost all cases you will be able to tell within three months whether someone is going to be suitable.

Grounds for an employee to take you to an industrial tribunal

Employment laws exist to protect both employer and employee. If an employee you have dismissed decides to take the matter to an industrial tribunal there is little you can do other than collecting together any evidence you have supporting your grounds for dismissal and preparing to fight your case on the day. If you lose, you may have to pay compensation to the employee you have offended (see page 185). You need to be aware of the reasons why you might be taken to a tribunal by one of your employees.

Unfair dismissal

Any employee who disagrees with your reasons for dismissing him or her can bring an action against you for unfair dismissal. The employee has no claim if she/he is guilty of one of the forms of gross misconduct outlined earlier in this chapter. However, an employee could justifiably claim unfair dismissal if dismissed because:

- she was pregnant
- she/he demanded legitimate rights such as a contract of employment, written terms and conditions of employment or pay slips, or asserted that certain deductions from her/his wages were illegal
- she/he pointed out to you certain health and safety hazards in your home.

A tribunal will also consider whether the employer thoroughly investigated the facts of the situation before making a decision to dismiss the employee. The employer may be guilty of unfair dismissal if:

- warnings were not given (in the case of anything other than gross misconduct)
- the employee did not get a chance to comment on the evidence (say, of theft or abuse of which the employee claims to be innocent)
- the decision to dismiss was made by someone with a minor involvement in the situation – for example, an elderly person

accuses a carer of theft and a relative who has not been involved in the care situation prior to that point makes the decision to dismiss the carer

- the employee did not get adequate notice of a disciplinary hearing
- an appeal was decided by someone who had already been involved.

A tribunal can ask an employer to reinstate or re-employ in similar work an employee who has been unfairly dismissed, but the employer has the right to refuse and pay additional compensation instead. Compensation takes several forms:

- basic – an award similar to standard terms of redundancy, dependent upon length of service and size of salary
- compensatory – an award equal to the loss of wages that the tribunal thinks is fair
- special – awarded only to employees who are dismissed for trade union reasons. A union representative can be involved in the compensation decision.

The tribunal can also reduce the amount of any award if it considers that an employee contributed to his or her dismissal by the way he acted or by his attitude.

Constructive dismissal

An employee's claim of constructive dismissal is generally based on the actions or behaviour of the employer. Complaints about employers' behaviour are covered further below. Actions taken by employers that have been deemed to constitute constructive dismissal by industrial tribunals include:

- reducing an employee's rate of pay
- completely changing the kind of job an employee does
- making an employee work outside her/his normal working hours.

In both unfair and constructive dismissal cases the tribunal will investigate whether or not an employer acted 'fairly' in dismissing an employee or causing him or her to resign. As far as the tribunal is concerned, acting 'fairly' means the employer acted reasonably in the circumstances.

For example, Employer A, a widower with two small children, employs live-in Nanny B. The contract of employment states that Nanny B will get three evenings off each week, as well as one full day at the weekend. Employer A runs his own business. It hits a bad patch, forcing him to work all the hours he can to rectify the situation. He explains this to the nanny but she takes umbrage at the fact that she is not getting her allotted time off and leaves. She subsequently claims constructive dismissal, alleging that her employer broke the terms and conditions of the contract. The tribunal, however, considers that Employer A acted reasonably in that he repeatedly apologised to the nanny and assured her that it would be a temporary situation; she was not prepared to compromise, and left. The tribunal found in the employer's favour.

Sex discrimination

The Sex Discrimination Acts 1975 and 1988 made it illegal to discriminate against workers on the grounds of sex or marital status. It is mainly women who take up issues under the legislation, although some male nursery nurses/nannies have brought claims of unlawful discrimination in employment processes. The Acts apply to self-employed as well as PAYE employees, provided any work is carried out under a personal contract for services (i.e. not through a contractor such as an employment agency).

An employer can fall foul of the legislation in the following ways:

- direct discrimination, whereby an employer treats a female employee less favourably than a man (or *vice versa*)
- indirect discrimination, whereby an employer applies an unnecessary requirement or condition, which is supposed to be equal for men and women but, in fact, affects only women (e.g. no separate changing or toilet facilities)
- pregnancy-related dismissals: no employer can sack anyone or make anyone redundant on the grounds of pregnancy or childbirth. It makes no difference whether the worker is full- or part-time or how long she has worked for you. The only possible defence is where an employer can legitimately assert that an employee's pregnancy means she is incapable of doing the job

and that to continue to do so is a risk to her health. This might be the case, for example, if you discovered that the care attendant who has to lift your elderly relative in and out of bed and perform other heavy-duty tasks several times each day was pregnant

- victimisation: if someone in your employ takes action against you under the Sex Discrimination Acts and you make her suffer for it – for example, by reducing her hours or her pay – you will be guilty of victimisation

- instruction/pressure to discriminate: it is unlawful to instruct or put pressure on others to discriminate against workers on the grounds of their gender

- aiding unlawful acts: anyone who knowingly conspires to discriminate against a worker is treated as though he/she had committed the act himself/herself. Therefore, employment agencies are careful to tell employers that they will provide staff only if the job complies with all necessary and relevant employment legislation.

- liability of employers: an employer is responsible for any of his/her staff who may commit an offence under the Sexual Discrimination Acts, even if the employer did not know about it or sanction it.

Sexual harassment

Sexual harassment is not covered by the Sex Discrimination Acts but is usually classed as direct discrimination and dealt with accordingly. For a male employer it can be a very difficult accusation to counter as in most cases it is the employee's word against the employer's. Prevention is better than cure: do not give an employee any reason to accuse you of sexual harassment (see Chapter 7). If you are unsure about the communication between you and your employee, ask another employee or a friend to be present during your discussions.

If the employee making a complaint against you can produce no witnesses this will weaken her case. Neither will it help her case if she has failed to follow the correct grievance procedure by putting her complaint in writing to you (see page 174).

Should you lose a sexual harassment or discrimination case, the tribunal can order you to pay the employee compensation (the amount is at the tribunal's discretion); less severely, it may order you to pay the employee's expenses and recommend that you change the practices that discriminate against employees.

It is possible to appeal against the decision of an industrial tribunal, but only on a point of law.

CASE HISTORY: Jamilla and Sundeep

Jamilla and Sundeep, both busy GPs, employed a full-time live-in housekeeper. The woman was from Germany but spoke excellent English. Sundeep is a naturally jovial man and was always informal and jokey with her when he was at home. He would often eat a meal in the kitchen, chatting to the housekeeper, when his wife was at work. To his amazement, she left one day while they were both out, leaving a letter saying that he would be contacted by her solicitor. She left no forwarding address. Soon afterwards, Sundeep was accused of sexual harassment and was summoned to a tribunal. It transpired that the woman thought he was making sexual overtures towards her. She accused him of persistently making suggestive comments, telling rude jokes and pestering her with his unwanted attentions. As all of this was supposed to have taken place whilst his wife was at work, Jamilla could not contribute to his defence in the matter. Sundeep denied any such behaviour and, after the tribunal had examined all the evidence, it came to the conclusion that it was probably a misunderstanding based on cultural and language differences. However, the incident caused Sundeep and Jamilla a great deal of anguish and dominated nearly a year of their lives. They now employ a woman from their own cultural background and Sundeep is extremely careful about his contact, behaviour and attitude towards the new employee.

Racial discrimination

The Race Relations Act makes it unlawful for anyone to discriminate against someone on grounds of race. As with sex discrimination, racial discrimination can take the form of direct or indirect discrimination. 'Race' is defined within the Act as colour, race, nationality or ethnic or national origins. Religion is not covered by the Act but can fall under one of the other headings: the term 'Jewish', for example, describes both a race and a religion. In Northern Ireland, discrimination on grounds of religion *is* illegal.

Employment in a private household is excluded from the Act (see Chapter 8), but you will find that any agencies with which you have dealings – employment, private home-care nursing, Social Services and so on – will abide strictly by the Race Relations Act. Should you persistently harass or discriminate against agency employees on the grounds of race or colour, however, you could find yourself hauled before an industrial tribunal. At the very least, you will find that agencies will be unable to provide you with staff because they themselves would fall foul of the law on the grounds of racial discrimination.

Discriminatory advertisements are unlawful, too, even if they are for jobs in a private homes (see Chapter 4).

Using an arbitration service

Should you have a dispute with an employee, even if you employ only one part-time domestic, you are entitled to ask ACAS to arbitrate for you to try to prevent the dispute escalating until it reaches a tribunal, review body or court. The approach to ACAS can be made by either party in a dispute. An industrial tribunal will automatically inform ACAS of a pending action and ask it to conciliate in an effort to settle the dispute and thus prevent it having to come before the tribunal.

You could also ask an employment agency to arbitrate in a dispute between you and an employee that the agency has provided. If the dispute is between you and an agency, you could ask the umbrella organisation to which the agency belongs to arbitrate (see 'Disputes with an agency', page 192).

A dispute between you and a contractor that threatens to come to court will automatically be referred for arbitration by the court as long as both parties agree. If one party does not agree the matter will proceed through the formal legal channels.

Whatever form it takes, arbitration is a useful way of getting an independent assessment of the problem and a fresh perspective, which may be able to resolve matters to everyone's satisfaction.

Disputes with public bodies

What can you (or your dependent relative) do if you consider that you are receiving inadequate or unreliable help at home from a public body such as Social Services, a local authority or the National Health Service? The procedure for bringing a complaint against such bodies is explained below.

Disputes with Social Services

Under the terms of the NHS and Community Care Act 1990, each Social Services department in the UK must inform all of its clients about its complaints procedure.

Included in the documents that accompany your care plan and contract should be a named person who is your point of contact on the first stage of the complaints procedure. This person is charged with trying, in the first instance, to resolve the problem through discussion or some form of action. Should this be unsuccessful, or should the designated person fail to respond to your verbal complaint, the second stage of the procedure will be to send a formal letter to that person outlining your complaint. The regulations state that you should see some action and an explanation within 28 days, and a report of the department's findings in relation to the problem within three months.

If you are dissatisfied with the report of the findings, you have up to 28 days from receipt of the report to ask to have your problem reviewed by a panel. This panel must be made up of at least three people and chaired by someone who is independent of the organisation being investigated.

Should all the measures above fail to produce an outcome that is satisfactory to you, you could try one of the following:

- contacting your local councillor
- contacting an influential support group such as Age Concern or Help the Aged
- contacting your local MP
- contacting the Local Government Ombudsman.

Disputes with a local authority

Should you consider that a local authority has a duty to provide you with a service at home but it is refusing to provide that service, or if it has withdrawn a service that you consider to be essential, two courses of action are open to you after you have exhausted the official complaints procedure with no favourable result:

- appeal to the Secretary of State for Health★
- appeal to a court.

Appeal to the Secretary of State for Health

The Local Authority Services Act 1970 (as amended by section 50 of the National Health Service and Community Care Act 1990) allows for an individual, or someone acting on that person's behalf, to report the local authority to the Secretary of State for Health, after going through the official complaints procedure.

The Act states: 'If the Secretary of State is satisfied that any local authority has failed, without reasonable excuse, to comply with any of their duties which are social services functions, he may make an order declaring that authority to be in default of the duty in question.'

In other words, if the appeal is successful, the Secretary of State will order the council to provide, upgrade or reinstate the service in question.

Court appeals

You can, in theory, sue a local authority for a breach of its statutory duty or ask for a judicial review of the local authority's actions to see whether the council has acted legally and reasonably. If you are on a low income you might qualify for legal aid. If your case is a landmark one that has implications for a number of other people, you may be able to get the support of a national action group. However, be aware when instigating such action that no legal procedure involving a public body is going to be anything other than slow and frustrating.

Disputes with the NHS

If you wish to make a complaint to the NHS regarding your eligibility to receive NHS continuing care at home after your discharge from hospital; or if your GP and the health authority are in dispute over your needs; or if there is a problem with the quality of care that you are receiving, you will have to follow the NHS complaints procedure. Details of the procedure are available from your local NHS trust or health authority, from the NHS Freephone Helpline or from your local community health council.

The usual sequence of events is, first, to make a written complaint to the local hospital, surgery or clinic in question. If this fails to resolve the matter you should ask the relevant NHS trust or health authority for a review of your complaint. Your request will not necessarily be granted, however. If that is the case, you will then have to contact the Health Service Ombudsman,* who has the power to investigate all complaints about care and treatment throughout the NHS system. An approach to the ombudsman must be made within one year of your starting the complaints procedure.

Disputes with an agency

As mentioned elsewhere in this book, when selecting an agency to find you a nanny, mother's help, au pair, nurse, carer or any kind of

---

FRES complaints and disciplinary procedure

FRES plays an important role in raising and setting standards in the recruitment and staffing industry. Part of this is to investigate complaints against members brought by clients, candidates, temporary and contract workers, and other relevant parties.

The FRES complaints/disciplinary procedure set out below should be considered in conjunction with the FRES Code of Good Recruitment Practice and, where applicable, with the code for the relevant specialist section.

(1) Where a complaint exists against an FRES member, that complaint should, in the first instance, be raised with a member firm – preferably in writing. If no satisfactory response or explanation is provided, a complaint may be brought to FRES.

(2) Complaints should be submitted in writing, addressed to the Commercial and Legal Adviser. Complainants should be asked to provide relevant documentation with their letter.

(3) A copy of the complainant's letter, together with any other relevant document, is forwarded to the named contact at a FRES member firm (not sent to a branch office) to enable the member to investigate and comment on the complaint. A letter should also be sent to the complainant informing him/her that a definite response will be sent as soon as possible.

---

domestic help, it is wise to choose one that is a member of an umbrella organisation (see Chapter 4). This provides two important benefits in the event of any dispute between yourself and the agency: first, the umbrella organisation can act as an independent arbitrator and perhaps help to resolve the dispute; second, should its arbitration efforts fail, you then have recourse to the umbrella body's complaints and disciplinary procedure. As an example of how such a procedure might operate, the box below cites the complaints and disciplinary procedure of FRES.

Before contacting an umbrella organisation, the first step to take in any dispute with an agency is to put in writing to the agency the nature of your problem or dispute. A letter or fax is acceptable, but

---

If there is any doubt as to whether the complainant would consent to a copy of his/her letter being forwarded to the FRES member, such consent must be obtained before a copy of the complainant's letter is forwarded to the FRES member. If the complainant will not give permission, a paraphrase of the letter should be prepared and sent. The member should be asked to reply within 10 days.

(4) The correspondence should be diarised on a weekly basis to ensure that the FRES member responds to the request to investigate and respond to the complaint. Members should always be asked to respond in writing.

(5) Upon receiving a response from the FRES member, the Legal and Commercial Adviser may contact both the complainant and the FRES member to seek further information or clarification on any matters raised.

(6) The Legal and Commercial Adviser will make a decision on the matter (if necessary having referred to the Chief Executive).

(7) If the complaint appears to have been resolved (e.g. payment made) both parties should receive a letter stating that this appears to be the case and that no further action is proposed. If appropriate, the member concerned should be advised on how the problem might be avoided in the future. If the complainant is not satisfied he/she should be told that the matter can be submitted to the Ethics and Disciplinary Committee, which will consider the complaint.

---

email is not as you will need a 'hard copy' of the original letter to show to an arbitrator or at a disciplinary hearing. You should cite in the letter or fax a deadline by which the agency must respond. If it fails to respond by the deadline you should instruct the agency (again in writing) that you intend to refer the matter to a lawyer or to the agency's parent organisation, which could be either the agency's head office or the relevant umbrella organisation to which it belongs. If this elicits no response, carry out your threat.

An umbrella organisation should have a formal complaints procedure. If the organisation does not get a satisfactory response from its member it will take the matter before an internal disciplinary committee or a review board. The outcome of such an investigation should be one of the following:

- the board cannot find a case to answer
- the complainant cannot provide sufficient evidence to prove that there is a case to answer
- the member should be reprimanded and asked to make redress to the complainant
- the member should be suspended from membership for a certain period or until redress is made
- the member should be expelled and the complainant advised to take formal legal action

Disputes with a contractor

As with an agency, it will help in the event of any dispute if the contractor you have employed is a member of an umbrella organisation. In practice, however, the majority of sole operators and small businesses that you will be employing in the domestic services sector are unlikely to be members of such an organisation.

The advice for hiring contractors is the same as for agencies or individual staff: write out a detailed specification of the work to be done, check references (to reassure yourself that a contractor has satisfactorily undertaken similar work before), agree terms and conditions before the job starts, and have a written agreement that you can both work to.

The complaints procedure, again, is similar to that for an agency. Write to the contractor outlining your complaint and set a deadline for reply. If that deadline is not met, send a letter, by recorded delivery, demanding immediate action and specifying the steps you intend taking to recover the money or, if applicable, to have the work re-done by someone else with the bill being sent to the defaulting contractor. If this still fails to elicit a response and the amount outstanding or in dispute is less than £3,000 (£750 in Scotland) you can pursue your complaint through the small claims procedure in the county court.

Small claims procedure

First, get a form from the county court and fill in the details of the claim/dispute, as well as any interest on the amount outstanding that you intend to claim. (You will also be given a booklet explaining how the small claims procedure works.) A fee of approximately 10 per cent of the claim is paid to the court when proceedings start. The court serves a summons on the contractor, providing that he or she lives within the area covered by your county court. The contractor then has 14 days in which to pay the full amount owed, make an offer of (for example) payment by instalments, or deny the claim. If the contractor does nothing, you have the right to have a judgment made in default, which means that the court will try to extract payment from him or her. If the contractor denies the claim a date for a hearing will be set, at which the claim in dispute will be considered.

This is not the end of the matter, however, as it is the responsibility of the plaintiff (i.e. you) to get the contractor to pay if the court has found in your favour. You therefore have to apply to the court for an enforcement order. A court has a variety of means at its disposal to make the contractor pay, such as making him or her sell some goods to raise the necessary funds.

Disputed claims of over £3,000 (£750 in Scotland)

If you are in dispute with a contractor who has caused you substantial financial loss you will need to consult a lawyer immediately, armed with the relevant evidence to support your case. If, for example, a specialist cleaning company had assured you that it had the necessary expertise to clean your valuable Persian rugs, then proceeded to ruin them, you would need to produce a copy of the contract that stated clearly the work to be done, photographs of the ruined carpets and, if possible, a written report from an independent specialist stating that the carpets were completely ruined because they had been cleaned using the wrong substances.

Act quickly

As emphasised throughout this book, prevention is far better than cure where employer/employee disputes are concerned, which is why it is so important to exercise a great deal of care in the recruitment of an individual or contractor; then, with luck, you may never need to resort to the sorts of measures described in this chapter. When something does go wrong, however, act quickly, and make sure that you document every step of the grievance or complaints procedure so that you are fully prepared in the event of the dispute reaching the tribunal or court stage.

Addresses and further reading

Advertising Standards Authority
Brook House, 2 Torrington Place,
London WC1E 7HW
Tel: 0171-580 5555
Fax: 0171-631 3051
Advice on the law regarding the wording of
advertisements

Advisory, Conciliation and Arbitration
Service (ACAS)
Brandon House, 180 Borough High
Street, London SE1 ILW
Tel: 0171-210 3613
Fax: 0171-210 3645
Web site: www.acas.org.uk
Provides advice, literature and practical support
in employment arbitration matters. Contact
your regional ACAS officer through your local
JobCentre or Department of Employment office

Age Concern Cymru
4th Floor, 1 Cathedral Road, Cardiff
CF1 9SD
Tel: (01222) 371566
Fax: (01222) 399562
Email: general@accymru.demon.co.uk

Age Concern England
Information and Policy Department,
Astral House, 1268 London Road,
London SW16 4ER
Tel: 0181-679 8000
Information line: 0800 731 4931
Fax: 0181-679 6069
Email: infodep@ace.org.uk
Web site: www.ace.org.uk
Produces a large range of helpful publications,
statistics, reports and factsheets relating to the
care of elderly people

Age Concern Northern Ireland
3 Lower Crescent, Belfast BT7 INR
Tel: (01232) 245729
Fax: (01232) 235497

Age Concern Scotland
113 Rose Street, Edinburgh EH2 3DT
Tel: 0131-220 3345
Fax: 0131-220 2779
Email: acs@ccis.org.uk

Association of Independent Care Advisers
58 Southwick Street, Brighton BN42 4TJ
Tel: (01483) 203066
Advice on care, care management and
monitoring. List of members available

The British Council
English Teaching Information Unit
10 Spring Gardens, London SWIA 2BN
Tel: 0171-930 8466
Fax: 0171-839 6347
Email: education.enquiries@britcoun.org
Web site: www.britcoun.org
Provides free copies of the Arels Felco guide to private language schools which are attended by au pairs

British Red Cross Society
9 Grosvenor Crescent, London SWIX 7EJ
Tel: 0171-235 5454
Fax: 0171-243 6315
Email: information@redcross.org.uk
Web site: www.redcross.org.uk
Information on services provided (such as the Home from Hospital schemes)

BTEC Information Service
Stewart House, 32 Russell Square,
London WC1B 5DN
Tel: 0171-413 8400
Fax: 0171-393 4445
Web site: www.edexcel.org.uk
Information about childcare qualifications

CACHE (incorporating NNEB and CEYA)
8 Chequers Street, St Albans,
Hertfordshire AL1 3XZ
Tel: (01727) 847636
Fax: (01727) 867609
Web site: www.cache.org.UK
Information about childcare qualifications

Carers National Association
20–25 Glasshouse Yard, London ECIA 4JS
Tel: 0171-490 8818
Fax: 0171-490 8824
Email: internet@carersuk.org
Web site: www.carersuk.demon.co.uk
Produces reports, statistics and publications relating to the problems of those caring for dependent relatives

Chiltern College
16 Peppard Road, Caversham, Reading
RG4 8JZ
Tel: 0118-947 1847
Fax: 0118-946 3218
Email: info@chilterncollege.com
Internationally recognised nanny college

Choice Publications
Apex House, Oundle Road,
Peterborough, Cambridgeshire PE2 9NP
Tel: (01733) 555123
Fax: (01733) 312025
Publishes advice for the elderly and some advertisements relating to care

CIETT (International Confederation of Temporary Work Businesses)
142–144 Avenue de Tervuren Bte
B-1150 Brussels, Belgium
Tel: 00 322 735 8230
Fax: 00 322 735 4412
Email: eva.casado@eppa.com
Web site: www.ciett.org
Produces a list of national employment organisations which are members of CIETT

Commission for Racial Equality (CRE)
Elliot House, 10–12 Allington Street,
London SWIE 5EH
Tel: 0171-828 7022
Fax: 0171-630 7605
Web site:
www.open.gov.uk/cre/crehome.htm
Advice on all aspects of the law relating to racial equality

Contact the Elderly
15 Henrietta Street, London WC2E 8QH
Tel: (0800) 716543
Fax: 0171-379 5781
Email: hq@contact-elderly.demon.co.uk
Web site: www.contact-the-elderly.org
A charity which provides various services for the elderly such as shopping, transport etc.

The Continence Foundation
307 Hatton Square, 16 Baldwin Gardens,
London EC1N 7RJ
Tel: 0171-831 9831
Fax: 0171-404 6876
Email:
continence.foundation@dial.pipex.com
Web site: www.vois.org.uk/cf
*Information, advice and literature on coping
with incontinence*

Continuing Care Conference (CCC)
12 Little College Street, London
SWIP 3SH
Tel: 0171-222 1265
Fax: 0171-222 1250
*Publications, reports and statistics relating to the
care of elderly people*

Contributions Agency
(Social Security advice line for
employers) (0345) 143143
Information about National Insurance matters

Crossroads
Third floor, Dilke House, Malet Street,
London WCIE 7JN
Tel: 0171-637 1454
Fax: 0171-463 5549
Email: cross1@dircon.co.uk
*Charity which provides practical support for
carers. Literature on services available, together
with details of local branches*

Daycare Trust
4 Wild Court, London WC2B 4AU
Tel: 0171-405 5617
Fax: 0171-831 6632
Email: daycaretrust@pop3.poptel.org.uk
Advice and publications on childcare issues

Eagle Star Insurance Co Ltd
The Grange, Bishops Cleeve,
Cheltenham, Gloucestershire GL52 4XX
Tel: (01242) 221311
Fax: (01242) 221554
Web site: www.eaglestardirect.co.uk

Equal Opportunities Commission (EOC)
Overseas House, Quay Street,
Manchester M3 3HN
Tel: 0161-833 9244
Fax: 0161-835 1657
Web site: www.eoc.org.uk
*Publishes reports, statistics and publications
relating to statutory rights and parents at work*

**Federation of Recruitment and
Employment Services (FRES)**
36–38 Mortimer Street, London
WIN 7RB
Tel: 0171-323 4300
Fax: 0171-225 2878
Email: info@fres.co.uk
Web site: www.fres.co.uk
*The national organisation for employment
agencies. Publishes lists of member agencies in
its various divisions, e.g. general employment,
caring, nursing. Copies of its Code of Practice
and Disciplinary Procedures are also available*

Greater Manchester Low Pay Unit
23 New Mount Street, Manchester
M4 4DE
Advice line: 0161-953 4024
Fax: 0161-953 4001
*Advice to employers and employees. Pay
factsheets and other information available*

Guardian Insurance Ltd
Civic Drive, Ipswich, Suffolk IPI 2AN
Tel: (01473) 212422
Fax: (01473) 230900
Web site: www.gre.co.uk

**Health Service Ombudsman (Health
Commissioner for England)**
Millbank Tower, Millbank, London
SWIP 4QP
Helpline: 0171-217 4051
Fax: 0171-217 4000
*Deals with complaints about the NHS that
have not been dealt with satisfactorily at a local
level*

Help the Aged
St James's Walk, London EC1R OBE
Tel: 0171-253 0253
SeniorLine (free national advice and
information service): (0800) 650065
Fax: 0171-250 4474
Email: hta@pipex.dial.com.uk
Web site: www.helptheaged.org.uk
*Publishes reports, statistics and publications
relating to the care of the elderly*

Home Office
Immigration and Nationality Directorate
Lunar House, 40 Wellesley Road,
Croydon, Surrey CR9 2BY
Tel: 0181-686 0668
Fax: 0181-760 1181
Web site:
www.homeoffice.gov.uk/ind/hpg.htm
*Advice, documentation and information on all
aspects of employing foreign nationals*

Inland Revenue
(contact your local area office for advice:
see telephone directory)
Web site: www.open.gov.uk/inrev
Information about tax matters

Institute of Employment Consultants
Third floor, Stewart House, 16A
Commercial Way, Woking, Surrey
GU21 1ET
Tel: (01483) 766442
Fax: (01483) 714979
Email: iec@iec.org.uk
Web site: www.iec.org.uk
*Members are individual consultants, most of
whom run agencies. Institute can supply
information about procedures and standards of
employment consultants*

International Au Pair Association
(IAPA)
UK representative
Sandra Landau
Childcare International Ltd, Trafalgar
House, Greville Place, London NW7 3SA
Tel: 0181-959 3611
Fax: 0181-906 3461
Email: mailbox@iapa.org
Web site: www.iapa.org
*Members of IAPA seek to promote best practice
and procedure in the field of au pair placements.
List of members and guidelines available*

International Butlers Association
Hellouwlaan 36, 4006 XJ, TIEL,
Netherlands
Tel: 00 31 344 673937
Fax: 00 31 344 673938
Web site: www.butlersguild.com
*Trains and represents butlers from all over the
world. Also advertises jobs*

The Lady *magazine*
39–40 Bedford Street, London
WC2E 9ER
Tel: 0171-379 4717
Fax: 0171-497 2137
Advertisements for and by domestic staff

Local Government Ombudsman
21 Queen Anne's Gate, London
SWIH 9BU
Tel: 0171-915 3210
Fax: 0171-233 0396
*Deals with complaints about local authority
services that have not been dealt with
satisfactorily at a local level*

National Childminding Association
8 Masons Hill, Bromley, Kent BR2 9EY
Tel: 0181-466 0200
Fax: 0181-290 6834
Email: 101450.2727@compuserve.com
*Provides information, publications, support and
advice to registered childminders and their
clients*

Norland College
Denford Park, Hungerford, Berkshire
RG17 OPQ
Tel: (01488) 682252
Fax: (01488) 685212
Email: mail@norland.co.uk
Web site: www.norland.co.uk
Internationally recognised nanny college

Norwich Union plc
PO Box 6, Surrey Street, Norwich
NRI 3NS
Tel: (01603) 622200
Fax: (01603) 683659
Email: helpdesk@norwich-union.co.uk
Web site: www.norwich-union.co.uk

Nursery World *and* Professional Nanny *magazines*
Admiral House, 66–68 East Smithfield,
London E1 9XY
Tel: 0171-782 3000
Fax: 0171-782 3131
Information and advertisements relating to nannies

Parents At Work
45 Beech Street, London EC2Y 8AD
Tel: 0171-628 3565
Publishes reports, publications and advice for working parents seeking to organise childcare

Personal Investment Authority (PIA)
1 Canada Square, Canary Wharf, London
E14 5AZ
Tel: 0171-538 8860
Fax: 0171-418 9300
Regulates the sale of most insurances and investments to the general public. Advice on long-term care insurance policies

Princess Christian College
26 Wilbraham Road, Fallowfield,
Manchester M14 6JX
Tel: 0161-224 4560
Internationally recognised nanny college

Professional Association of Nursery Nurses (PANN)
2 St James's Court, Friar Gate, Derby
DE1 1BT
Tel: (01332) 343029
Fax: (01332) 290310
Email: pannpat.org.uk
Web site: www.pat.org.uk
Advice and literature on the standards for professional nannies and nursery nurses

Professional Nanny *magazine: see* **Nursery World**

Qualifications and Curriculum Authority
29 Bolton Street, London W1Y 7PD
Tel: 0171-509 5555
Fax: 0171-509 6666
Email: info@qca.org.uk
Web site: www.crownbc.com/qca
Information about childcare qualifications

Royal Association for Disability and Rehabilitation (RADAR)
Unit 12 City Forum, 250 City Road,
London ECIV 8AF
Tel: 0171-250 3222
Fax: 0171-250 0212
Web site: www.radar.org.uk
Information and literature on subjects of interest to people with disabilities, including Social Services provision

Secretary of State for Health Department of Health
Richmond House, 79 Whitehall, London
SWIA 2NS
Tel: 0171-210 3000
Fax: 0171-210 5523
Web site:
www.open.gov.uk/doh/dhhome.htm
Deals with complaints concerning failure of duty by a local authority

United Kingdom Home Care Association (UKHCA)
42b Banstead Road, Carshalton Beeches, Surrey SM5 3NW
Tel: 0181-288 1551
Fax: 0181-288 1550
Represents private care agencies and can supply Code of Practice, sample contract, and other useful information

Working for Childcare
77 Holloway Road, London N7 8JZ
Tel: 0171-700 0281
Fax: 0171-700 1105
Useful information and practical advice for working parents trying to organise childcare

Yours *magazine*
Apex House, Oundle Road, Peterborough PE2 9NP
Tel: (01733) 555123
Fax: (01733) 312025
Advice for the elderly and some advertisements on care matters.

Further reading

Caring for Someone at Home by Gail Elkington and Jill Harrison
Available through bookshops or the Carers National Association (see above)

Choosing a Childminder: A Guide for Parents
Available from the National Childminding Association (see above)

Daily Telegraph Guide to Long Term Care by Ian Cowie
Available free from:
PPP Healthcare, Elm Court, Stratford-upon-Avon, Warwickshire CV37 6PA
Tel: (0800) 585059

The Working Parents Handbook (a practical guide to the alternatives in childcare)
Available from Parents At Work (see above)

Index